"I can readily say that your work is most impressive, with new and insightful information that is clearly based on extensive research and considerable thought. It doesn't feel puffed up as if you are working hard to stretch out your material, but leaves the reader with the feeling, as a work should, that the author hasn't exhausted himself on the subject by laying on the reader every possible word and extrapolation. A very strong effort to put together a book that is significant, fascinating, and readable and that shows a remarkable degree of scholarly research." R. K., RKEdit

"I found the book enticing and was so fascinated with it that I actually read the whole thing in two days! I could not put it own! I am constantly sharing the information with others. Thank you again." E. G.

"Those of us, whom the Lord God has opened our ears to hear, and our eyes to see, will recognize immediately the leading of the Spirit in this writing. Do not think it is a book like those sensationally-titled ones you see at your super-market; you will not find this author proclaiming himself "specially" or "mysteriously" informed about End-time prophecy. Instead, you will find the author to have been diligent, questioning, and open to the truth of our Savior. If you've ever had your own personal questions that seemed unanswered by religious dogma or church doctrine, this is the one book you should not miss."
El Besino (http://elbesino.wordpress.com)

"Outstanding! Jonathan

Also by Zahyit

Oil for the Lamps
How to Overcome Religious
and Spiritual Deception or
The Importance of Being Victorious
During Our Lifetime

Kabbalah: End-Age Mysticism
Mystical Secrets Hidden in the Hebrew Language
or How to Achieve Spiritual Mastery
as We Come to the End of Our Age

PROPHECY UNSEALED!

The Great Destiny of Human Kind as
Prophesied by the Scriptures

or

How to Prepare for
the Coming New Age

BY ZAHYIT

Innertech Publishing
Laguna Niguel, California

Copyright © 2007 - 2008 by Timothy J. Sakach, Ph.D.
All rights reserved.

Published by Innertech Publishing
PO Box 7560, Laguna Niguel, California 92607

Web: ElahimConnection.com

"Lift Up Your Voice" Blog:
Innertech.WordPress.com

No part of this publication may be reproduced, stored in a retrieval system or transmitted, in any form or by any means, electronic, mechanical, photocopying, recording, or otherwise, without the prior permission of Innertech Publishing. Unless otherwise stated quotes from Scripture are from the New International Version. The author reserves the right to substitute names from the original language and to emphasize words and phrases in Scriptural passages.

Keywords: History, Prophecy, Revelation, Spiritual, Scriptures, Prophets, End Age, Resurrection, Enoch, Daniel, Ezekiel, Zechariah, Malachi, YHWH

ISBN: 0-934917-04-3
EAN: 9780934917049
Ver: 1.2

Manufactured in the United States of America

Contents

Dedication	7
Acknowledgments	8
Preface	9
Introduction	11
How To Use This Book 12	
The Blessing of Enoch	15
Use of Proper Names	16

"CLOTHED WITH THE SUN"

1   Among Hidden Prophecies   19

2   The **Revealed** Calendar   23
    1 Enoch, Chapter 72: 23; Major Trouble Changes the Earth 27; The Earth Sped Up 28; Earth's Atmosphere Damaged 29; Pulling the Life-Terminating Trigger. 30; Like a Skater's Pirouette 31; Earth's Rotation is Not Constant 32; Lifespan Shortened by Hundreds of Years 33; We Have a Revealed Calendar: Why? 33

3   Visions of Ages to Come   35
    Enoch's Vision of the Ages 35; **Week 1:** Enoch's Time 35; **Week 2:** Noah's Time and the Flood, Nimrod 35; **Week 3:** Abraham 35; **Week 4:** Moses and the People of Israel 36; **Week 5:** Temple Built 36; **Week 6:** Captivity of Eyahudim to Babylon 36; **Week 7:** Age of Apostasy, World religions 36; **Week 8:** Kingdom of God (Elahim) established on earth. First Resurrection, Millennial reign 37; **Week 9:** Second Resurrection 37; **Week 10:** Angels judged. Earth and heaven pass away. New Heaven and New Earth created 37; **Many weeks to come:** Eternity 38; A Prophecy Debunker's Dilemma 38; Sixth Week 39; Seventh Week 39

4   The Sixth Age: Blindness   41
    The Prophecies of Enoch 41; Prophetic Objectives 43; Know and Understand 46; Polluted and Impure Bread 48; The 69 Weeks 49; The Seven Weeks/Years War 51; "Confirming a covenant with the mighty ..." "Sacrifices Cease!" Daniel 52; "The people of the ruler destroy the city and the sanctuary," Daniel 53; "The House of Dominion shall be burnt with fire," Enoch 53; The city rebuilt with streets and a trench ... 54; The Coming of the False Messiah 54; The 69 **Literal** Weeks! 57; Simeon Bar-Kokhba: Son of the

Star 60; The Mystery of the Missing "Week" 61

5 The Seventh Age: The Great Apostasy   **63**

How Apostasy Starts 63; Deception: The Hallmark of Apostasy 64; The Paul Problem 64; Take a moment and make this prayer your own: 74

6 Feasts, High Days, and the Revealed Calendar   **75**

Service Schedule for Priests Assigned to 364-day Year 77; The Placement of the Feasts and High Days 77; The Holy Year, Quarter 1, According to Scripture 78; 1 78; Feasts and High Days of the First Month 79; The Passover Feast 79; The Feast of Unleavened Bread 81; The Feast and High Day of the Third Month 82; Jesus' Death and the Passover 83; The Feasts & High Days of the Seventh Month 84; The Problem of Keeping the Sabbath and the Feasts 86

FROM HERE TO KINGDOM COME!

7 An End For Our Age   **93**

Physical Calendars 93; "Signs in the Sun and Moon" 95; Wars and Battles Between Nations 96; Signs in the Planets 96; Target Earth! 97; The Prophetic Revealed Calendar 98; The Woman Clothed with the Sun 99

8 Revisiting Daniel's Visions   **101**

Enoch's Calendar: the Key to Prophecy 101; Daniel's Messages from Gabriel 102; Daniel 9: The End of the Sixth Age 104; Daniel's Ninth Chapter and the 70 Weeks 104; Daniel 12: More End of the Age Prophecies 105

9 Forward to the End   **107**

Daniel 10: The target of the revelations 107; Daniel 11: Crossing troubled waters 108; Daniel 12: Events close the Seventh Week 110

10 Like Pieces of a Puzzle   **113**

Clues given to Daniel and John 114; Believe it or not, these words are about to be unsealed. 115; John's visions and the Secret of Elahim 116; Two witnesses prophesy for 1,260 days 118; Who are the two witnesses? 118; The last three and one half years of the seventh age 119

11 The Day of the Living One   **121**

Feasts, High Days and the Revealed Calendar 122; When is the real Sabbath day? 123; Spiritual turmoil in heaven and earth 124; The Day of Eyahuwah (He Who Exists) 125; Events leading up the Day 126; Summary of the Last Seven Years 127; Waiting for the

End of the 1,335 Days 128

12 **The 1,335th Day**   *129*

The last seven years of our age and beyond 130; Signs tied to ALL the descendents of Jacob 131; Why know about this special time of the end? 131; A new Temple or Tabernacle and Altar in Jerusalem? 132; What happens at the end of the 1,335 days? 133; What is significant about that day? 133; The Torah Speaks of That Day 135

13 **The Fulfillment of Day 1,335**   *137*

The 1,335 Days Prophecy Revealed 137; The Two Wave Loaves 140

"BEHOLD, MY BELOVED!"

14 **"In the Image of God"**   *145*

Now we know what we shall be 147; Mary's conception: How it happened. 149; The Birth of the Sons of Elah 150

15 **"We Shall Be Like Him"**   *151*

"He who exists" or "The Living One" That is the Name 151; Mystical Resources 153; Raised to Reality and Awareness 154; Message to the Churches: 155; Message to Judah: 156; Prophecy says "יהוה" is Coming to Earth" 156

Epilogue   *161*
References   *163*
BLOG: "Lift Up Your Voice!"   *166*

Comments from Readers of the Blog: 166

Dedication

To my Father who "begat" me and provides for me; and to my Mother who carries me, teaches me, feeds me, comforts me, and gives me Life.

Both my father and mother died 91 days apart while I wrote this book. My father praised and served God until the day he died. My mother earnestly prayed from an early age that God's will be done in her life. It was. She died laughing.

Acknowledgments

I am very pleased to offer heartfelt thanks for the comfort, encouragement, and counsel and support that I received from my wife and companion, Marina. She also wants me to thank our two cats, Olga, and Murzik – the talking cat. Really, his "good morning" greeting is always a good way to start the day.

I appreciate the talks that my daughter Suzanne and I shared about the writing of this book and what it meant to our lives. And thanks to my sons Stephen for his help and support. I also want to thank my friends and neighbors who encouraged me to hang tough and see the book through to the end.

And special thanks to Ron Kenner of RKEdit of Los Angeles whose editing insights and experience helped make the message of this book free of my own weaknesses.

Preface

It is an awe-inspiring experience to realize that I have a part in writing a book that contains a message whose time has come. I found that many people fear addressing these prophecies and what they hold for our frightening time. That I can offer hope to many was one of the main forces behind the research and the writing. The good news within these pages is light years above any bad news that accompanies it. The bad news is temporary. The good news is eternal, and that is why this book exists.

In a world threatened by religious tyranny, this book shows you how you can achieve spiritual freedom and power. Those who threaten your spiritual freedom are themselves slaves to the deadly power of religion. In the end they will not prevail. This book contains knowledge that makes this promise a great reality: *"Now a slave has no permanent place in the family, but a son belongs to it forever. So if the Son sets you free, you will be free indeed!"* Read on and understand.

Introduction

This book provides material to help anyone understand sealed and unknown prophecies about a period of time called "the end of the age." Although I started writing about the mystery of the 1,335 days of Daniel's vision, I found myself in a fascinating place, as many mysteries were solved before my eyes. Research into these mysteries suggested the discovery of the most important events yet in the history of the human race!

These events answer the great questions:

Why were you born?

What is your ultimate destiny?

Who are you?

This book will take you into territory you never expected to visit.

I believe that you, like many, sense something huge will happen in the near future. In the face of daily bad news, it often seems that the world is getting ready for a great change. At least, it should get ready.

"What I say to you, I say to everyone: 'Watch!'" Mark 13:32

The recent discovery of long lost scriptures and the solving of old and hidden mysteries shows this to be a time of great opportunities.

1. New revelations and knowledge, not available before, are now there for those who search for them. You will find deep peace and lasting hope by knowing the truth about your future!

2. I am not proposing a new religion. Nor do I attempt to proselytize or induce you to join anything. But should you understand what this book contains, you will rediscover Life.

3. This book reveals passages of the Scriptures where the understanding remained hidden until this time. Now, at last, you can experience and understand the real story of the Scriptures and of your great future.

4. What if you "can't" believe what you will be reading? You have a choice:

continue reading and see if it makes sense at the finish, OR don't read it, in which case you will not know, until the fulfillment comes and then you will understand. These prophecies do not depend upon whether or not you believe or even know about them. But if you understand this message now, then according to the prophecy, you are among "the wise and the knowledgeable," a good place to be.

How To Use This Book

One of these mysteries focuses on events that happen at the end of a stipulated time of 1,335 consecutive days. To understand this mystery, you need to know when to start counting the days and what to expect to find at the end.

Our time was determined long ago to be *the time* to finally know the true meaning not only of the 1335 days but also the prophecies that accompany it. With that knowledge you can begin now to prepare yourself for your great future.

To understand this mystery you need some information:

First, you need a calendar. Not just any calendar will do. You cannot take one off your wall and expect it to contain any clues relating to this mystery. Our common calendars do not have a clue about anything of any importance to your future or mine. These awkwardly counts days, seasons (somewhat), and shows us when our "important" days come, like Thanksgiving, Tax days, Christmas and Easter, and when our new year begins and so on. And God forbid that we should miss a holiday with a three-day weekend!

Second, you need to know about special days that tell about your future. You will see how the Law places these days on the special calendar. We cannot use our current calendars because they make nonsense out of these special days and it is foolish to try to place them there. But these days do make sense when combined with the right calendar. Then we recognize that any other calendar is man-made.

Third, you need to understand the revealed outline of the history of the human race. There is a prophetic vision that will help you understand the special time in which you now live. If we do not live in the time of the unsealing of this message, then I am guilty of wasting your time trying to solve this mystery, because at only one time in the history of humanity can we find the solution. Then, afterward, the knowledge will remain forever.

Fourth, given these historic times, we must focus on our current age.

We will discover:
> Its importance in history
> What it means to live in this age
> The good and bad about it

Fifth, you will need to know about world-wide events and conditions that will exist at the end of our age. If you understand the special calendar with special days fixed in their proper places, then you can know when the counting starts and what great events happen at the end of the 1,335 days.

Sixth, you will see that you can successfully identify the start and end of the 1,335 days. Then you can begin to understand its importance not only for you but also for the rest of the world. And nothing could be more worthwhile and rewarding!

Seventh, you will find out what makes the 1,335 days special for you. It is the day the world waits for – even though it has no idea this day even exists. You will learn why this day was singled out and made a mystery to be solved NOW. And, most importantly, you will find out why this is important for you!

You have a choice, to understand and participate, or to wait and watch it happen and realize then what you missed. If you wait you may regret it. But in spite of that, you will still be able to rejoice and look forward to the future with great hope! You may not find this new material anywhere else. It is highly controversial, because many people invested in established traditions upon which they based their religion. This is an authoritative answer to prophecies hidden for millennia to be revealed at this time and only this time.

So, as you read, relax and let the words speak to you.

You also need to free yourself from "sacred cows" and clean your mind from biased thinking. We all have things we think are important to us, but in reality some things imprison our minds. These came from our parents, teachers, political leaders, traditions, friends, enemies, advertisements, religious teachers including some who claimed to be apostles, motion pictures, books, music, media, news reporting, and from our own head. Some of these "dear" things came with threats of peril to life and limb, "God will get you, if ..." Others came with sweetness, pleasantness, and deception. Even our own ideas can often be our worst enemies: "Wow! I just had a great idea" can often lead to trouble.

But remember, if deep down inside you really want to know the truth, then "you will know the truth and the truth will set you free."

That is a promise! And so we begin ...

> **People**, from Hebrew אלקים "whom God resurrects" Proverbs 30:31. "A *King* in the company of His *People*." (A prophetic passage long considered unintelligible.)

Says the Lord of Spirits: "And in those days shall the earth also give back that which has been entrusted to it, and Sheol (the grave) also shall give back that which it has received, and hell (also the grave) shall give back that which it owes.

"For in those days the Chosen One shall arise, and shall choose the righteous and holy from among them, for the day draws nigh that they should be saved.

"And the Chosen One shall in those days sit on My throne, and his mouth shall pour forth all the secrets of wisdom and counsel." Enoch 51:1-3

"And יהוה [Eyahuwah (Lit. - He exists!)] shall be King over all the earth." Zechariah 14:9

The Blessing of Enoch

The words of the blessing of Enoch, wherewith he blessed the elect and righteous, *who will be living in the day of tribulation*, when all the wicked and godless are to be removed.

And he took up his parable and said, "Enoch, a righteous man, whose eyes were opened by God, saw the vision of the Holy One in the heavens, which the angels showed me, and from them I heard everything, and from them I understood as I saw, *but not for this generation, but for a remote one which is to come.*

"The Holy One will come forth from His dwelling, and *the Eternal God will tread upon the earth.*"
1 Enoch 1:1-4

Use of Proper Names

Where possible, in this book, I will refrain from using the words Jew, Jews or Jewish, *unless they apply to the material, traditions, and practices that came from post-exilic apostasy.*

When referring to the Nation and the People of Judah, I will, out of respect, use *Eyahudah* and *Eyahudim* (plural). These names more correctly show the close association between the People of Eyahudah and the Savior: Eyahuwah (יהוה). The Hebrew name of Jacob's fourth son means: "Let Eyahuwah (יהוה) be praised."

In the same way I will use *Eyahushuah,* to refer to the one we call "Jesus". The name means "*He who exists* is our Savior."

Eyahuwah (יהוה) or "He who exists" or sometimes when refering to Himself, "The Living One" is the One who created Adam and Eve, made the covenants with the Fathers from Adam through Abraham, Isaac, and Jacob, with the nations that descended from them, and with King David. Eyahuwah also spoke to the Nation and the people of Israel in the Spirit through the Prophets. He was dead, but now lives for ever and ever. (From Revelation 1)

I

"Clothed with the Sun"

Understand the Times

And a great sign was seen in heaven: a woman clothed with the sun, with the moon under her feet, and on her head a crown of twelve stars. Revelation 13:1

1   Among Hidden Prophecies

The last chapter of the book of Daniel in the Hebrew Scriptures contains a special prophecy. The messenger who gave him this prophecy told him it was sealed until a time called the "time of the end".

Daniel did not write about the end of the *earth and all life on it*.

Not at all!

Other prophecies show "the end" is not the end of our planet, but rather the end of an age. Daniel received information from a messenger (angel) about the end of one age and the beginning of the next.

Meet Enoch.

Enoch was the seventh generation from Adam and Eve. He is also the father of all the people who now live on the earth. He was the great-grandfather of Noah, who is also the father of us all. During Enoch's life he found he had special tasks given to him from God to take information and pass it on to the ages to follow, and in particular, to our age, to his descendants living at this time. As you will read, Enoch wrote books of information given to him by messengers in the same way the message below was given to Daniel, and to the other prophets, like Ezekiel, Isaiah, and to John the Apostle

The Apostles in the first century CE quoted from Enoch's books and Enoch's words are part of the New Testament. Copies of Enoch's books were also found among the Dead Sea Scrolls. In his writings Enoch also prophesied that his books would become known at a time far beyond his time. They were for future generations. Moses knew what he was to do because of Enoch's visions.

Enoch received a vision about human history and how it was to be divided into periods of time called "weeks." In the vision, the messenger showed Enoch that humans were given seven "weeks" before the "change" would come. The seven "weeks" are seven distinct ages. These are marked with events that happen during each age. As each age ends another starts immediately. Enoch wrote the second age would include the time of the "first end." This end came as a result of a great flood. But human life continued on.

Daniel also wrote the vision given to him about events to happen at the close of the seventh age and the beginning of the eighth. Both Enoch and Daniel saw a great transformation or change marking the end of the seventh age and the beginning of the eighth age. We live during the time when the seven ages, which Enoch saw in a vision, will be completed.

Concerning the events of this time, here is one of the prophecies given to Daniel by the messengers from Elahim. Here is Daniel 12 from the Jewish Study Bible:

> At that time, the great prince, Michael, who stands beside the sons of your people, will appear. It will be a time of trouble, the like of which has never been since the nation came into being. At that time, your people will be rescued, all who are written in the book.
>
> Many of those that sleep in the earth *will awake*, some to eternal life, others to reproaches, to everlasting abhorrence.
>
> And the knowledgeable will be radiant like the bright expanse of the sky, and those who lead the many to righteousness will be like the stars forever and ever.
>
> But you, Daniel, **keep the words secret, and seal up the book until the time of the end.** Many will range far and wide and knowledge will increase.
>
> Then I, Daniel, looked and saw two others standing, one on one bank of the river, the other on the other bank of the river. One said to the man clothed in linen, who was above the water of the river, "How long until the end of these awful things?"
>
> Then I heard the man dressed linen, who was above the water of the river, swear by the Ever-Living One as he lifted his right hand and his left hand to heaven: "For a time, times, and half a time [3 and 1/2 years]; and when the breaking of the power of the holy People comes to an end, then shall all these things be fulfilled."
>
> I heard and did not understand, so I said, "My lord, what will be the outcome of these things?"

He said, "Go, Daniel, for *these words are secret and sealed to the time of the end.* Many will be purified and purged and refined; the wicked will act wickedly and none of the wicked will understand; but the knowledgeable will understand.

"From the time the regular offering is abolished, and an appalling abomination is set up — it will be a thousand two hundred and ninety [1290] days.

"Happy is the one who waits and reaches one thousand three hundred and thirty five [1335] days.

"But you go on to the end; you shall rest, and *arise to your destiny at the end of the days.*"

What you are about to read contains the explanation of this prophecy and the other prophecies of Daniel and other Scriptures that pertain to the time of the end of our age and of the age about to come. These reveal that we live in a unique time in the history of the human race.

> **Note:** I will be using Hebrew words to explain some scripture passages and theological concepts. There is no greater language on earth than Hebrew for theological understanding. Nothing even comes close. For example, Greek has only one word for a supreme Power: theos, from which we get "theology". But in Hebrew there can be hundreds of words to describe what we weakly refer to by the single word: "God."

2   The *Revealed* Calendar

Enoch, a man of Elahim (the Almighty Ones), lived prior to the great flood that happened during the time of his great-grandson Noah. Enoch's calendar is the most mysterious calendar of all, because it is the only *revealed* calendar. The revelation is recorded in one the Books of Enoch called the Book of Luminaries. According to Enoch, the Messenger Uriel gave this revelation to him. Uriel commissioned Enoch to write this knowledge and pass it on to the generations to come including our generation.

In this chapter, we will examine Enoch's calendar to see its structure, the events controlling it, and whether or not it makes sense to use it. We need a calendar we can use to not only answer questions about the 1,335 days but also any other prophetic periods of the Scriptures.

Both spoken and written word carried the revelation of Enoch's calendar through the ages. Researchers found Enoch's books among the Dead Sea Scrolls, with copies of Enoch's writings dating earlier than 200 BC. In 1773 J. Bruce, an "Indiana Jones" Scottish explorer, found copies of the Book of Enoch in Ethiopia and ran back to England with a few copies.

The recurring solar events that you read about here are important to Enoch's calendar; a knowledge of these events is essential to help you understand our time. You will also learn why the 1,335 days of Daniel's prophecy make our time one of the most life-changing times in history.

1 Enoch, Chapter 72:

I will only quote the prelude to this chapter and show a chart of the months and their times and durations as given to Enoch.

> The book of the courses of the luminaries of the heaven,
> the relations of each, according to their classes, their domin-
> ion and their seasons, according to their names and places

of origin, and according to their months, which Uriel, the holy angel [messenger], who was with me, who is their guide, showed me.

And *he showed me all their laws exactly as they are, and how it is with regard to all the years of the world and unto eternity, till the new creation is accomplished which endures till all eternity.* Enoch 72

In other words, whether or not we know anything about it or even believe it, *this calendar is still valid today* and will continue until the New Heavens and New Earth are created!

Here are things you need to know about this calendar:

    The start of the year

    The length of the months

    The events marking the start of each of the quarters

    The structure and length of the year

    And any other calendar laws

The following table summarizes much of this information from Enoch's writings:

Month	Length	Starting Event (Day 1)
1	30	Spring Equinox (Start of Quarter 1)
2	30	
3	31	
4	30	Summer Solstice (Start of Quarter 2)
5	30	
6	31	
7	30	Fall Equinox (Start of Quarter 3)

Month	Length	Starting Event (Day 1)
8	30	
9	31	
10	30	Winter Solstice (Start of Quarter 4)
11	30	
12	31	

Total number of days in the year is 364.

This is the actual number of days, during Enoch's time, between consecutive spring equinoxes. The equinoxes are simply the two days in the spring and fall of the year when the length of the daytime equals the length of the nighttime. These days identify the beginning of spring and fall. On our calendar the spring equinox occurs about March 21 and the fall equinox about September 22.

Two days in each year mark the occurrence of the solstices. In the summer the solstice occurs about June 21. This is the day when the daytime is the longest and when the nighttime is the shortest during the year. This day we call the beginning of summer. About December 21 the winter solstice occurs, when the daytime is the shortest and the nighttime the longest during the year. This day marks the beginning of our winter.

In the revealed calendar all of these solar events mark the beginning of each quarter. And to keep the calendar in line with the solar events, an intercalary day is added at the end of each quarter, rather than adding extra days to the end of the year.

Unlike our calendar, these solar event days are always the first day of the month and of each quarter, *and they always fall on the fourth day of the week.* The calendar starts on the middle day of the week because in Genesis 1 time reckoning started on the middle or fourth day of the week when the sun, moon and stars were set for days, seasons and for signs. And all days start and end at sunset, not at midnight.

On Enoch's calendar, the day of the spring equinox is the "New Year's Day." The relation of this calendar to the equinoxes and solstices assumes great import and carries the calendar through to our day, even though we may not know about it.

Notice that each period of three months is a quarter and is 91 days long. Each quarter is exactly 13 weeks long, and unlike the Aztec and Egyptian calendars, there is no five-day period at the end of the year. Instead, as noted, an intercalary day is added at the end of the last month in each quarter and thus the total number of days is 364. This structure is significant.

Because the length of our year is more than 365 days, some great event must have occurred to cause this change, as we shall see

Enoch recorded the revealed calendar and showed that it is based on laws that could not be ascertained by natural observation *during our time*. He wrote for the generations to come and to establish it as a witness to his offspring for all time. Because during the time of his grand-children the natural conditions of the earth changed, and about that change, Enoch gave this warning:

> In respect to the days of the sinners, the seasons are cut short. [The 364 days comes before the solar year is complete.]
>
> Their seeds shall lag behind in their lands and in their fertile fields, and in all their activities upon the earth. He will turn and appear in their time and withhold rain, and the sky will stand still at that time. Then the vegetable shall slacken and not grow in its season, and the fruit shall not be born in its proper season.
>
> The moon shall alter its order, and will not be seen according to its normal cycles. In those days it will appear in the sky and it shall arrive in the evening in the extreme ends of the great lunar path in the west. And it shall shine more brightly, exceeding the normal degree of light.
>
> Many of the chiefs of the stars shall make errors in respect to the orders given to them; they shall change their courses and functions and not appear during seasons, which have been prescribed for them. All the orders of the stars shall harden against the sinners and the conscience of those that dwell upon the earth. They (the stars) shall err against them (the sinners); and modify all their courses. Then they (the sin-

ners) shall err and take them (the stars) to be gods.

And evil things shall be multiplied upon them; and

plagues shall come upon them, so as to destroy all. Enoch 80

This calendar is based upon the positions of the earth, sun, moon and stars as they were before the flood. So what *we* see is not what we should be seeing if the earth was still in sync.

I brought this to a researcher who studied viruses and molecular machines. She told me that a change of as little as 5 minutes per day in the rotation speed of the earth was sufficient to cause problems with crops, weather patterns, and the way the human "machine functions". The human body and all life on the earth is affected by the relationships between the sun, the moon and the stars. The five minutes per day accumulates and, over time, alters the relationship of the earth to the moon and stars. More about this later.

Major Trouble Changes the Earth

Powerful changes altered the relationship between the earth, sun, moon and stars. But only one change had power enough to confuse the way people calculated the calendar. Some time during the time of human history, a little more than one day was added to each year. One event caused this change.

Now, when the earth completes 365 exact days around the sun, it is short 0.242 days from where it was 365 days ago. So every four years we add another day to make up for that shortfall.

On Enoch's calendar the year comes up even shorter — 1.242 days shorter.

The orbit of the earth takes 365.242 days or 365 days and 5.808 hours. So even though we add a leap year of 24 hours every four years, we still need to skip a leap year periodically to make up for the shortfall of 46 minutes for each leap year.

An earth day is the time it takes for the earth to spin on its axis one time. Thus a year in days is the number of complete spins that the earth makes until it completes one orbit around the sun. Without relying on a clock, we can easily tell when the earth completes one day. *Simply watch the sun go down.* The time between consecutive sunsets is one day. And it is just as easy to tell when a new year ends and begins! *Watch for the equinox.* That is: watch for the time during the spring of the year when the shadow cast by a pole at sunrise points to the place on the horizon where the sun will set.

The Earth Sped Up

Some change added 1.242 days to the year. The rotational velocity of the earth is now 0.465 km/s or about 1040.47 miles per hour at the equator.

The mean orbital velocity (the average speed that the earth travels in its orbit around the sun) is 29.78 kilometers per second or about 66,666 miles per hour! A change in the number days required to complete a year (spring equinox to spring equinox), required a change in either the rotational speed or the orbital speed. Either the earth had to spin faster or the earth had to travel slower in its path around the sun. When the earth spins faster, more days will happen during a year and visa-versa.

Given that the orbital speed is more than 66 times greater than the rotational speed, the odds and "ease of change" are on the side of how fast or slow the earth spins or rotates. To go from 364 days in Enoch's time to 365.242 days in our time and to produce the additional 1.242 days, something had to increase the rotational speed of the earth! The amount of change required to in the earth's rotational speed to cause the number of days to increase from 364 to 365.242 is only about 5 feet per second!

> March 4, 2003, Goddard Space Flight Center
> CHANGES IN THE EARTH'S ROTATION ARE IN THE WIND
>
> "Because of the Earth's dynamic climate, winds and atmospheric pressure systems experience constant change. These fluctuations may affect how our planet rotates on its axis according to NASA-funded research that used wind and satellite data.
>
> "Angular momentum describes the rotation of the Earth around its axis ... A normal, 24 hour, day is based on the mean speed of the rotation of the whole Earth, including its atmosphere and ocean. **When the motions in these fluids move mass to different positions, the angular momentum changes in them and will affect the solid Earth rotation.**
>
> Given the rotation rate, fluid mass and distance from the Earth's radius, if one variable is changed, at least one other variable also must also change.
>
> For example, a spinning ice skater spins slower with extended arms and faster when his arms are pulled in. Simi-

larly, the spinning Earth is affected by many factors, including changes in the way the winds blow or currents in the ocean. *Some of these factors can act to speed the planet up, while others literally drag it down.* Of course these effects are very small, but observable by advanced scientific techniques."

CREDIT: NASA SVS, Jim Strong and Horace Mitchell

The biggest event prophesied during Enoch's time was the great flood. This event nearly killed all life on earth, except for one family and a select group of birds and mammals.

The revealed text tells us that Enoch's great-grandson Noah received the task of building a large enclosed ship or barge on dry land to provide a place of refuge during the flood. The flood was an "end-time-prophecy" and signaled the end of the "second week" or age in Enoch's prophecy. Enoch called it, "the first end."

It is possible that a natural event triggered the end of that age and completely changed the length of the year in days or from sunset to sunset.

EARTH'S ATMOSPHERE DAMAGED

The flood also changed the atmosphere of the earth by removing protective atmospheric layers. Increases in gamma ray exposure to the troposphere (our air) resulted in an increase in radiocarbon. Because carbon is an essential atom in our DNA base the addition of radiocarbon atoms into DNA resulted in shorter life span. When the radiocarbon in DNA reverts back to nitrogen, the DNA chain breaks apart releasing free radicals and producing cellular mutations.

The increase in radiocarbon after the flood also produced an anomaly in the radiocarbon ratio making the specimens of the time prior to the flood appear much older, by radiocarbon dating, than they really were. Less radiocarbon atoms in the ecosystem at the time the carbon based organism dies, results in an aberration in dates. The mistake lies in the assumption that the amount of radiocarbon then was the same as now. We have no proof that it was the same. But there is evidence that it was much less than it is now and that it took several generations after the flood for the amount of radiocarbon to stabilize.

Willard Libby, the University of California scientist who received the Nobel Prize for his discovery of radiocarbon dating by using radiocarbon to carbon ratios, warned that dates more than 5,000 years old could only be assumptions and were highly inaccurate:

> "The first shock Dr. Arnold and I had was that *our advisors informed us that history extended back only 5,000 years...* You read books and find statements that such and such a society or archaeological site is [said to be] 20,000 years old. We learned rather abruptly that these numbers, these ancient ages, are not known; in fact, it is about the time of the first dynasty in Egypt that the last [earliest] historical date of any real certainty has been established." Willard Libby, "Radiocarbon Dating," in *American Scientist*, January 1956, p. 107. [Libby was the one who pioneered the discovery of radiocarbon dating.]

Interesting! The Egyptian calendar also only goes back to the time of the first dynasty. The radiocarbon dates are also skewed because radiocarbon contamination had not yet stabilized, making even that time appear older than it really was.

But Enoch's calendar goes back before that time.

Pulling the Life-Terminating Trigger.

What caused the great flood is still unsolved. If a comet or asteroid struck the earth near the equator, it could have created a Life Terminating Event ("LTE"). If it came from a direction opposite to the orbit of the earth, and hit the earth on the side facing the sun, it could speed up the rotation of the earth like a whip striking a toy top.

Sometime in the recent past, a large object struck the earth near the Yucatan and left a crater 185 miles in diameter, large enough to be visible from the moon. At first examination some thought that the crater was 120 miles in diameter, but geologists found a ripple surrounding the site with a 185 mile diameter. The cause of such a large crater was an asteroid of about 6 miles wide, striking the earth at a speed of 45,000 miles per hour. But we must not forget that the earth was also traveling at 66,000 miles per hour giving a combined impact speed of 111,000 mph!

This is enough energy to destroy all life on the planet and focus energy through the earth's core and cause land masses to rise and fall, enormous volcanoes to spring up, and underground water streams to break through the surface. In addition, it would cause long-term atmospheric changes including rainfall that lasted for weeks and cloud coverage for months.

Like a Skater's Pirouette

Although the earth could have been struck by something, the evidence is difficult to nail down because of the problems inherent in dating methods and the interference to research based on preconceived notions about the history of the earth.

One event recorded in the Scriptures tells a different story. A cosmic event happened before any human beings lived on the earth.

Paul LaViolette in his book, *Earth Under Fire*, wrote that at times in earth's history, dust clouds from the center of our galaxy entered into our solar system. Deposits from ice core samples taken from Greenland verified this. From the point of view of the earth, the cosmic dust super wave would cause the moon to appear as blood color, the sun to grow dim, and the stars vanish from site. The lack of sun energy caused by cosmic dust clouds resulted in the ice ages and times of darkness on the earth. But when the sun began consuming the cosmic dust, it spewed tremendous heat into the solar system. This caused global conflagrations making the waters on the earth boil and separate. LaViolette wrote:

> The conflagration would have evaporated large amounts of water into the atmosphere.

After the cosmic dust cloud passed out of the solar system, the earth and even Mars had changed.

Genesis 1 tells of a great separation of the waters into waters above (in the stratosphere) and waters below (the oceans and lakes) with the sky or expanse (troposphere) in between.

> Now the earth was formless and empty, darkness was over the surface of the deep, and the Spirit of Elahim was hovering over the waters. And Elahim said, "Let there be light," and there was light. Elahim saw that the light was good, and He separated the light from the darkness. Elahim called the light "day," and the darkness he called "night." And there was evening, and there was morning—the first day. And Elahim said, "Let there be an expanse between the waters to separate water from water." So Elahim made the expanse and separated the water under the expanse from the water above it. And it

was so. Elahim called the expanse "sky." And there was evening, and there was morning—the second day.

The waters in the stratosphere provided a great shield to protect the earth from gamma and cosmic rays. This dense stratosphere would have minimized the creation of radiocarbon in the troposphere by *reducing* the energy of gamma rays: a process called *bremsstrahlung*.

In addition to stabilizing temperatures around the earth, the waters in the upper atmosphere would have had another effect on the earth. Like a skater holding her arms out during a pirouette, the water in our stratosphere would slow the rotation of the earth. But when the skater draw her arms closer to her body, her speed increases. When the masses of water in the stratosphere returned to the earth, its rotation speed increase.

Earth's Rotation is Not Constant

As late as the 1930s scientists believed that the earth spun at a constant and unchanging speed. But space scientists discovered that this was not true. The rotation speed did change. In fact, without entering the speed of earth's spin into their calculations, they found that they could miss the celestial targets.

NASA makes continual checks on the changes in rotational speed to accurately calculate the trajectory needed to launch space vehicles to specific targets outside of the clutches of earth's gravity. They know that weather alone can change the rotational speed of the earth.

The Book of Genesis records that the waters above the earth came back down causing the flood. From that time on, the earth has never been the same. When the waters came down, the earth reacted like an ice skater drawing her arms into her body. The earth's spin increased and added more days to the year. The number of earth days required to complete a solar year became 365.242.

The number of days in a year, from spring equinox to spring equinox increased to almost 366 days, and the atmosphere no longer protected future inhabitants from harmful radioactive materials – including radiocarbon.

Radiocarbon is produced in the upper troposphere by gamma rays striking nitrogen atoms changing them to radiocarbon or C14. This becomes part of our food chain and is present in the air we breathe. Because carbon is an essential element in building the DNA base, our DNA protein molecules are contaminated by radiocarbon. A naturally radioactive isotope of carbon has a presumed atomic mass of 14 with a presumed half-life of 5,780 years; this enables what has come to be known as the 'carbon 14 dating process,' given its use, as a tracer, in carbon dating. To determine dates with this method, scientists must know the level of radiocarbon saturation at the time of the specimens death.

Lifespan Shortened by Hundreds of Years

From these atmospheric changes one may presume that the human life span went from nearly 1,000 years down to 120 years or less depending on other conditions. Our bodies now give off 15 beta rays per gram of carbon per minute. Thus for each beta ray, another radiocarbon atom in a human body turned back to nitrogen, and very likely a DNA chain broke down threatening cellular mutations.

By studying progeria, the premature aging of infants, scientists discovered that the aging process found in babies and children was the same as that found in the elderly. Aging is the result of the breakdown of the DNA chain causing both mutations in DNA, the release of free radicals in the body, and faulty reconstruction of internal organs.

The increased amounts of radiocarbon in the atmosphere after the flood caused a rapid decline in the life span. This decrease started immediately after the flood and did not stabilize until about the time of Moses.

Psalm 90, A Prayer of Moses, tells of the shortness of our life of 70 years, or, if we are strong enough, we may live to be 80 years old:

"For all our days have *declined* in Your fury." Psalm 90:9
NAS

Declined? Our life lasts less than one tenth of the years our fathers lived! Medical scientists consider that under the best conditions, we can live to 120 years.

The Lord said, "My Spirit will not contend with man forever, for he is mortal, *his days will be 120 years.*" Genesis 6:3 NIV

The earth and all life on it changed dramatically after the flood. Evidence points to a major difference between the quality of life on the earth before the flood and afterward.

We Have a Revealed Calendar: Why?

Uriel revealed the calendar to Enoch and told him to preserve it for future generations before the change came. Enoch's offspring carried the information through the flood and preserved it for us. Without Uriel's revelation to Enoch, this calendar could not have been deduced from conditions after the flood. We do not have the wisdom nor the tools to discern the structure of Enoch's calendar given the present conditions. Yet, the laws of the calendar continue to endure throughout all time until the creation of the new heavens and earth.

Now we will begin to see why this calendar, in particular, is so important. We were given detailed information about it and its structure and it is time to learn why. No other calendar can help us understand prophetic statements and events – even though the calendar doesn't match with current conditions.

We also need to understand Enoch's other visions about future events to come upon human kind. Like the calendar, the entire outline of human history was revealed to Enoch in a vision.

We must understand this as well.

3   Visions of Ages to Come

The following prophetic vision reveals the history of human kind including the past, present and future. The vision contains two sections. The first section reveals the first seven complete "weeks" or ages. The second starts immediately after the first seven ages end and continues on without end. It is a vision of your future, whether you believe it or not. It is your future, even if you never heard about it before. This vision contains the prophecies about the age we live in now: the Seventh Age. This is Enoch 93 and was translated by R. H. Charles.

Enoch's Vision of the Ages
And Enoch began to recount from the books and said:

Week 1: Enoch's Time
"I was born the seventh in the *first week*, while judgment and righteousness still endured."

Week 2: Noah's Time and the Flood, Nimrod
"And after me there shall arise in the *second week* great wickedness and deceit shall have sprung up and *in it* there shall be *the first end*.

"And in it a man [Noah] shall be saved. And *after it is ended, unrighteousness* shall grow up and a law shall be made for the sinners."

Week 3: Abraham
"And after that in the *third week at its close* a man shall be elected as the plant of righteous judgment, and *his posterity*

shall become the plant of righteousness for evermore."

WEEK 4: MOSES AND THE PEOPLE OF ISRAEL

"And after that *in the fourth week, at its close,* visions of the holy and righteous shall be seen, and a law for all generations and an enclosure shall be made for them."

WEEK 5: TEMPLE BUILT

"And after that *in the fifth week, at its close,* the house of glory and dominion shall be built forever."

WEEK 6: CAPTIVITY OF EYAHUDIM TO BABYLON

"And after than *in the sixth week* all who live in it shall be *blinded,* and the hearts of all of them shall *godlessly forsake wisdom."*

Jesus (Eyahuwah/Eyahushuah), the Destruction of the Temple, and the Dispersion in 135 AD.]

"And in it *a man shall ascend;* and, *at its close,* the house of dominion shall be burnt with fire, and the whole race of the chosen root shall be dispersed."

WEEK 7: AGE OF APOSTASY, WORLD RELIGIONS

"And after that *in the seventh week* shall an apostate generation arise, and many shall be its deeds, and all its deeds shall be apostate."

Creation revealed, Intelligent Design revealed, Space Exploration, Quantum Physics.

"And, *at its close,* shall be elected the elect righteous of the *eternal plant of righteousness,* to receive sevenfold instruction concerning all His creation.

"For who is there of all the children of men that is able to hear the voice of the Holy One without being troubled? And who can think his thoughts? And who is there that can behold all the works of heaven?

"And how should there be one who could behold the heaven, and who is there that could understand the things of heaven and see a soul or a spirit and could tell thereof, or ascend and see all their ends and think them or do like them?

"And who is there of all men that could know what is the breadth and length of the earth, and to whom has been shown the measure of all of them?

"Or is there any one who could discern the length of heaven and how great is its height, and upon what it is founded, and how great is the number of the stars, and where all the luminaries rest?"

WEEK 8: KINGDOM OF GOD (ELAHIM) ESTABLISHED ON EARTH. FIRST RESURRECTION, MILLENNIAL REIGN

"And *after that there shall be another, the eighth week,* that of righteousness, and a sword shall be given to it that righteous judgement may be executed on the oppressors, and sinners shall be delivered into the hands of the righteous.

"And, *at its close,* they shall acquire houses through their righteousness, and a house shall be built for the Great King in glory for evermore, and *all mankind* shall look to the path of uprightness.

WEEK 9: SECOND RESURRECTION

"And after that, *in the ninth week,* the righteous judgement shall be revealed to the whole world, and all the works of the godless shall vanish from all the earth, and the world shall be written down for destruction.

WEEK 10: ANGELS JUDGED. EARTH AND HEAVEN PASS AWAY. NEW HEAVEN AND NEW EARTH CREATED

"And after this, *in the tenth week in the seventh part,* there shall be the great eternal judgement, in which he will execute vengeance amongst the angels. "And the first heaven shall depart and pass away, and a new heaven shall appear, and all the powers of the heavens shall give sevenfold light.

Many weeks to come: Eternity

> "And after that *there will be many weeks without number* for ever, and all shall be in goodness and righteousness, and sin shall no more be mentioned for ever."

Notice the big change that happens in the eighth week.

The use of the term "weeks" ties in with later prophecies concerning the end-times — the end of these "weeks" or ages. The "end time" always refers to the end of one of these ages! We are living during the close of the seventh week. Also the words "at it close" means the "end time." Each age ends with some significant important event.

Both Christians and Jews assume that 1000-year periods mark the ages and that we are in the sixth age. But there is no set time implied here. Each age ends with some significant important event. Nowhere does Enoch's vision imply 1,000 year periods. We live in the seventh age that started after the dispersion of the people at the close of the sixth age in 135 CE about 1,975 years ago.

A Prophecy Debunker's Dilemma

Some scholars and other's not so scholarly focus on prophecies like these with the intent to prove them false. Some say that prophets wrote the prophecies after the events happened. Otherwise, according to the scholars, how could the prophets know the future? So rather than admit that the scholars do not know how a prophet prophesies, they make the prophets appear to be liars. If that doesn't work, the scholars pull another trick out of their magic hat. They say the prophets, influenced by current events, only wrote the news of the day like journalists.

This prophecy of Enoch makes both tricks very difficult. Because this vision covers the history of human kind, where in the sequence can you place the prophet? And because this prophecy contains known events in the recent past and events yet in the future, the prophet must live and write for thousands of years!

To make matters even more difficult, recent discoveries unearthed copies of Enoch's writings known to be more than 2,200 years old that match other documents discovered in the 1700s. Among the Dead Sea Scrolls, 20 Aramaic copies of Enoch's manuscripts were buried in the first century CE and only uncovered recently. Copies of Enoch's books were found in 1773 in Ethiopia. Researchers compared the Ethiopian copies with the Dead Sea Scroll version 4QEng and found the documents matched with enough clarity to force the dating to as far back as 400 BCE

This means the prophet wrote about the end of the sixth week and the apostasy of the seventh week while they were yet in the future. These things did not happen during or before the time of the writer. He wrote about the future.

The temple was burned during the seven years war in the first century CE, and Romans dispersed the people of Judea in 135 CE after the failure of the uprising led by a false messiah called Simon Bar Kokhba.

And considering the accuracy of the prophecies and the current fulfillments at the end of this age, the seventh week, we cannot help but conclude that Enoch's book requires our attention. This is a book of prophecy.

We must look more closely at the prophecies of the sixth and seventh weeks. Their fulfillment 2,000 years ago and their continued fulfillment today impact every minute of our day.

SIXTH WEEK

Spiritual Blindness, a Man ascends, the Temple burnt by the people, and the people dispersed deeply changed our world. The strength of these events of first and second centuries CE in and around Jerusalem rocked the world then and set it upon a new course. Every one of the weeks of Enoch changed the direction of human history and shaped the world and its people to our time. Because our minds get so focused on triviality, we miss the important events.

SEVENTH WEEK

Great Apostasy still marches on.

The Plant of Righteousness, both people of Eyahudah and the Lost Tribes of the House of Israel at their present locations, unknowingly receive inspired knowledge about the creation. Knowledge like Intelligent Design, great cosmic events of the past, and the extraordinary creation of humankind attest to prophecy fulfillment. The prophecy foretold about space exploration accomplished by actually ascending into space and by using telescopes and contemplative physics.

Even though naysayers may cover their ears and shout "NO" very loudly, this changes nothing. Spiritually inspired knowledge will continue to gain strength until it covers the earth "like the waters cover the sea."

Despite the problems today, as well as living in an age of religious tyranny and confusion, we really live during the time in this age when we can *expect* to receive spiritual enlightenment.

To better understand our time and age, we must look deeper into what really happened during the Sixth and the Seventh Ages.

4 The Sixth Age: Blindness

Very close to the end of Eyahushuah's life his disciples came to him as he was leaving the Temple and called his attention to the buildings. Jesus turned to them and said, "Do you see all these things? I tell you the truth, not one stone here will be left on another; everyone will be thrown down."

The disciples then asked, "Tell us, when will this happen, and what will be the sign of your coming and of the end of the age?"

Jesus and the disciples walked from the Temple to the Mount of Olives just a short walk to the east. There, the gospels report, he disclosed to them a revelation of future events that would affect them *in their "age"* and would eventually *affect the whole of mankind at the close of the "next age."*

The ending and beginning of "ages" are major turning points in the history of humankind. Because the Sixth Week or Age of Enoch's vision ended as prophesied by Enoch, Daniel and Malachi, it is important to understand how the fulfillment took place. If we understand that, then we can look more clearly at what happened in our Seventh Week and how it will end.

Josephus, the historian, considered Daniel,

> One of the greatest prophets ... for the books that he wrote and left are read by us even now ... He not only predicted the future, like the other prophets, but specified *when events would happen.* (Ant 10.266-8)

As we shall see Daniel was given a message that portends very difficult and trying times for his people and for Jerusalem. The gospel writer of the Mount of Olives prophecy makes a direct reference to Daniel's words and encourages the reader to understand.

THE PROPHECIES OF ENOCH

Some, who are not willing to recognize Enoch, called "the scribe of righteousness", consider that Daniel's prophecy provided the material that was "borrowed" by the writer of Enoch. How can we accept such conjecture when it does not explain any future fulfillment of Enoch's other words?

The introduction to Enoch's Book Five states:

> Book Five, which is written by Enoch, the writer of all the signs of wisdom among all the people. He is blessed and noble in all the earth. It is written for all the *offspring* that dwell upon the earth, *and for the latter generation which uphold righteousness and peace.* Enoch 92:1

It is believed that the various writings of Enoch, perhaps over 300, did not exist in a grouped form until after the time of Ezra. The apocryphal (hidden) Fourth Book of Ezra, chapter 14, reported that the scriptures had been burned when Eyahudim were taken to Babylon, so Ezra in 40 days restored the scriptures with the help of a number of scribes and a miraculous memory recall.

> And when the forty days were ended, the Most High spoke to me, saying, "Make public the 24 books that you wrote first and *let the worthy and unworthy read them*; but keep the 70 that were written last, in order to give them to the wise among your people. *For in them is the spring of understanding, the fountain of wisdom, and the river of knowledge."* And I did so.

It appears that among those books had to have been the books of Enoch:

> In that place *I saw the fountains of righteousness,* which does not become depleted and is surrounded completely by *numerous fountains of wisdom.* All thirsty ones drink of the water and become filled with wisdom.
>
> Enoch 48:1 (Charlesworth)

The Old Testament is riddled with evidence of dictation, containing brief comments and references that could only come from scribal editing that seeks to bring the books "up to date." It wasn't until the time of the Septuagint in 285 B.C. that the books of our Bible were put into a single volume. Some versions of the Septuagint also included not only our common Old Testament but also the Apocrypha (hidden) books. The so-called "Pseudepigrapha", includes 1 Enoch, The Book of Jubilees, The Testament of the Patriarchs, and other important writings. Many were found among the Dead Sea Scrolls.

The influence of many of these can be seen in the writings of the apostles. The apostles treated Enoch's writings as revelation (Jude, 2 Peter 2), and so considered him a prophet. As shown earlier, The Books of Enoch contain prophecies, particularly the prophecies about the "weeks" or ages, that were fulfilled, are continuing to be fulfilled, and are yet to happen. Past events showed the fulfillment of Enoch's prophecies. But at the same time they transcend the entire span of human history. So we are forced to recognize the Book of Enoch as a principle key to knowledge and understanding.

Enoch even prophesied that his writings would be published again at the end of this seventh age! There are copies available from different sources, and there are complete copies from the Dead Sea Scrolls that have yet to be translated and published.

Prophetic Objectives

Many English translations of Daniel 9 show a lack of understanding combined with preconceived ideas. They even go so far as to corrupt the meaning of words. Traditional explanation of this passage tries to make everything apply only to Jesus. And that is just not correct. Here is the passage from Daniel 9 known as the "Seventy weeks prophecy":

> While I was speaking and praying, confessing my sin and the sin of my people Israel and making my request to the Lord my God {Eyahuwah Elahim] in behalf of the holy mountain of my God – while I was still in prayer, Gabriel, the man I had seen in the earlier vision, came to me in swift flight about the time of the evening sacrifice.
>
> He instructed me and said, "Daniel, I have now come to give you insight and understanding. As soon as you began to pray, an answer was given, and I have come to tell you for you are highly esteemed. Therefore, consider the message and understand the vision:
>
> "*Seventy weeks are decreed for your people and your holy city* to finish transgression, to put an end to sin, to atone for wickedness, to bring in everlasting righteousness, to seal up vision and prophecy and to anoint the most holy.
>
> "Know and understand this: From the issuing of the decree *to restore and rebuild Jerusalem* until the messiah, the ruler, comes, there will be seven weeks and sixty-two weeks. It will be rebuilt with streets and a trench, but in times of

trouble. After the sixty-two weeks, the messiah will be cut off and will have nothing.

"The People of the ruler who will come will destroy the city and the sanctuary. The end will come like a flood: War will continue until the end, and desolations have been decreed. He will confirm a covenant with the mighty for one week, but in the middle of that week he will put an end to sacrifice and offering. And one who causes desolation will place abominations on a wing of the temple until the end that is decreed is poured out on him."

It is important to point out the context in which this answer came to Daniel. Because this prayer is often ignored when studying this prophecy, so are the clues to understanding the answer.

"In the first year of Darius the son of Ahasuerus, of Median descent ... in the first year of his reign I, Daniel, observed in the books the number of the years which was revealed as the word of the Lord to Jeremiah the prophet for the completion of the desolations of Jerusalem, namely, *seventy years*."

If we are to conclude anything about what is meant by the word "weeks" in the answer, we have a clue that it might have something to do with "70 years." Here are the passages from Jeremiah that Daniel referred to:

This whole land [Judea and Israel and the nations about them] shall be a desolate ruin. And those nations shall serve the king of Babylon *seventy years*. Jeremiah 25:11

For thus said Eyahuwah, "*When Babylon's seventy years are over*, I will take note of you , and I will fulfill to you My promise of favor – to bring you back to this place." Jeremiah 29:10 NSB

Daniels prayer continues:

"Moreover, **we have not listened to your servants, the prophets, who spoke in your Name to our kings, our princes, our fathers, and all the people of the land.**"

The second problem is that these things came upon all the people because they, including their "messiahs" and "princes", did not hear or listen to all the warnings given by the prophets.

"Righteousness belongs to you, O Lord, but to us open

shame, as it is this day – *to the men of Judah, the inhabitants of Jerusalem, and all Israel, those who are nearby and those who are far away in all the countries to which you have driven them,* because of their unfaithful deeds which they have committed against you."

This prayer was not limited to only Judah, who were also called the "Jews", but it covered all of the tribes and people of Israel wherever they were – around the world. All "Jews" are Israelites – but not all Israelites are Jews! This distinction is missed by even the most "learned" of all Biblical "scholars"!

The word "week" in the translation means a "seven". One "week" means one period of something. "Seven weeks" means seven of something. "Sixty-two weeks" means sixty-two of something. Also, one lone "week" is not addressed directly. Just what that "something" is must be determined. And a "week" can also mean "a year!" The use of the word "week" also has specific prophetic significance as we shall see later.

"The holy mountain" is Jerusalem. This is made clear by Daniel's prayer that makes up the first section of the ninth chapter.

The prophecy of Daniel 9 reveals that a period of time, called "seventy weeks" or "seventy sevens" (or, if not pronounced correctly, it could also mean "seventy seventy") has been set aside for the following purposes:

- To finish transgression
- To put an end to sin
- To atone for wickedness
- To bring in everlasting righteousness
- To seal up vision and prophecy
- To anoint the most holy

These things happen to Daniel's people, the House of Judah, to the House of Israel where ever they are in the world, and to Daniel's holy city, Jerusalem. The prophecy also contains a set of very specific events concerning people, rulers, sacrifices, and abominations.

According to the record, Daniel had just recalled the prophecies of Jeremiah concerning desolations on Jerusalem (Jeremiah 25:11-12; 29:10). Seventy years had passed since all those things began to happen. Daniel felt moved to confess the sins of his people and to cry over the destruction of Jerusalem and the desolation of the sanctuary.

Immediately, Gabriel, a spiritual messenger, was sent to give Daniel a message in response to Daniel's supplications and to encourage Daniel to understand the vision Gabriel had given him earlier.

The time to accomplish all those things listed above was given as "70 weeks." Now the first thing that most students of prophecy do is to multiply those 70 by 7 giving 490, which could mean 490 days. Then they extrapolate that to years. So they assume that this is referring to a period of 490 years and nothing more.

Unlike the instructions given to Ezekiel, nowhere in this prophecy are any instructions that Daniel should count a day for a year and consider each "week" as a 7 year period.

On the contrary, the context of the prophecy of Jeremiah that Daniel had been reading talks about 70 *years*! But the Hebrew or Chaldean in which Daniel wrote uses the plural for the word for "seven" or "week" instead of the word for "year" as in Jeremiah. This is the phrase in Hebrew:

שבעים שבעים נחתך

The plural for "seven" is spelled the same as the word for "seventy." That causes uncertainty in the translation and allows for Daniel's words to use all of the meanings contained in the word translated "weeks" or "sevens;" that is: *a single week, seven days, seven years,* or even *a week for a year* following Jeremiah's *seventy years*! The words mean "seventy sevens" are to **be cut, divided or intersected.**

The interesting choice of words will require wisdom and understanding as we view the meaning of the prophecy in the context of its fulfillment. As we shall see, the 70 "sevens" or "weeks" will be *intersected* or cut into pieces when they are applied to the people of Israel.

Know and Understand

Daniel was told that 70 "weeks" were intersected *on the people and on the city* for the accomplishment of those things. Daniel was also told to "Know and understand this".

When the gospel writer referred to this prophecy, he said,

> "So when you see standing in the holy place the abomination that causes desolation, spoken of through the prophet Daniel – let the reader understand – then let those who are in Judea flee to the mountains." (Matt. 24:15.)

One thing that ought to be clear is that context of Jesus' Mount of Olives prophecies refers to events affecting Jerusalem, Judea, and the people, and the end of, at least, that age!

What Daniel was told to "know and understand", and what Jesus said the reader of Daniel should "understand", was apparently something that people could understand. The encouragement to understand contains the possibility that *understanding* was possible. This means that the prophecy is open, at least to the wise, and not hidden, as is the case with Daniel 8 and 12, which was sealed until the end of our age. Some of what was told to Daniel was "sealed until the time of the end." But not this passage.

Now, let's understand it. To do so we must take each prophetic statement and find where it fits into the historic record of that time. Daniel's prophecy uses a grammatical device called "hyper-baton". This means that the sequence of events is not found in the natural order given by the written record (in other words, like an overly active conductor's baton). Nostradamus used this same device in his writings. Therefore, like a puzzle, we have the pieces, but they have to be connected properly. Then, when assembled, all should become clear.

To what we have already listed above, here are the remaining pieces.
- A decree was to be given to *restore and rebuild Jerusalem*. [not the Temple]
- 7 *weeks* and 62 *weeks after the decree* a messiah or "anointed one", a prince [ruler, captain] would come. Note: this is only 69 of the 70.
- Jerusalem would be rebuilt with streets, and trenches (moats, conduits, or even latrines), in times of trouble.
- After 62 weeks, the "anointed" one will be cut off and he will have no one or nothing left.
- The people of the ruler who will come will destroy the city and the sanctuary.
- The *end will come* like a flood.
- The war will continue *until the end* and desolations have been decreed.
- He (the ruler) will confirm a covenant with many (or "the mighty") for *one week*.
- In the midst of that week, he will put an end to the sacrifices and the offerings (cause them to cease).

- The one who causes desolations (makes desolate) will come on the wings of abominations, until the desolations that have been decreed are poured out.

It seems strange that after Daniel had been praying about Jerusalem, the desolations, the destruction of the temple, the sins of his people and all the people of Israel, he received a prophetic vision about future troubles. Like Enoch, Daniel's visions and prophecies also transcend time and cover ages!

Let's now examine the historical events that surrounded the destruction of the temple and Jerusalem, and in fact, all of Judea.

POLLUTED AND IMPURE BREAD

Daniel prayed about the restoration of Jerusalem and about the problems of his people. But it had become obvious that the people were not going to change their ways in spite of the fact that they had been severely disciplined.

Enoch prophesied that when the people returned from captivity they would build the temple, and "place a table before [it], but all the bread [spiritual food] on it was polluted and not pure".

Such was the case, after the return, Ezra and Nehemiah and the prophets tried to restore the people, but were continually harassed by all kinds of problems.

- Priests divorced and intermarried with the native women.
- The people stopped paying the tithes.
- Major changes took place in the religion of the people;
- The foundations of Phariseeism and Judaism were laid and the Law replaced.
- The revealed solar calendar was rejected .
- They abandoned the Jubilee Year.
- They substituted the Babylonian lunar calendar and months and devised schemes to maintain the feasts in their relationship to the moon.

As a consequence of all this, they became "blind." There was problem with the post-exilic adoption of the Babylonian calendar and the people abandoned Enoch's revealed calendar.

The devout keepers of the Dead Sea Scrolls maintained both the lunar and prophetic ("revealed") calendars so that they could keep watch on the times and the events. Jesus and his life followed the Feasts in accordance with the times on the prophetic calendar. (John 7:1-14)

Daniel's prayer petitioned for a genuine change in the hearts of the people. He said they were called by God's name, and for the sake of God's faithfulness, he pleaded for His intervention. The answer came immediately.

Eyahuwah Elahim saw that those who bore His name and did wickedly caused His holy Name (character) to be blasphemed among the nations. This happens even today! He determined that they now faced a time of reckoning, atonement, and dispersion!

- There was coming a time of desolation so that the world would no longer look upon them as a nation, in particular, a nation of God.
- He would remove his Temple by allowing it to be destroyed.
- He would bring desolations upon the people allowing them to be driven from the land.
- He would make an end of the transgression.
- He would make an atonement (sacrifice) for wickedness.
- He would bring in everlasting righteousness.
- All of this to happen within a span of 70 "weeks"!
- And it would happen to his people (the Jews) and to Jerusalem.
- But future fulfillments could include all of the people of Israel wherever they are in the world – not just the Jews.

THE 69 WEEKS

The 70 "sevens" time of Daniel 9 is divided (intersected, cut up) into at least three sections and further subdivided into smaller sections..

The first is the declaration of the 70 weeks. The second is a detailed description of 69 of those weeks. This is divided into two sections one 7 "weeks" long and one 62 "weeks" long. The third is a very significant one "week" section.

And don't forget, the most likely definition of a "week" is one year. However, we shall see that the word "sevens" has other meanings as well. Let us now put the puzzle together.

Jesus referred to the prophecy of Daniel 9 in the Olivet prophecies. In answer to the question asked by the disciples, Jesus, or at least the writer of the gospel applied the prophecy to Judea, to the temple, and to the end of that age.

However, there is another prophecy linked directly with the end of that age and with the end of our age. As we saw according to the Book of Enoch, the time of human existence was divided into periods of varying length also called "weeks". Enoch's time was the "first week." The time of Jesus and the apostles was the sixth week, a time of great blindness on the people.

> "And in the sixth week all who live in it shall be blinded, and the hearts of all of them shall godlessly forsake wisdom" (1 Enoch 93:8).

There are many references to their blindness in the words of Jesus and in the epistles. In addition to the blindness, Enoch was told of three highly significant events that would happen during the sixth week:

- "And in it, a man shall ascend;"
- "And at its close the House of Dominion shall be burnt with fire,"
- "And the whole race of the chosen root shall be dispersed."

These last two occur *at the end of the sixth "week" – at the end of that age*. This was a puzzle to the disciples. Some were convinced that Jesus would return at the end of the "sixth week" of Enoch's revelation. However, another distinct age of Enoch, had yet to come – the Age of Apostasy.

> "And after that in the seventh week shall an apostate generation arise, and many shall be its deeds, and all its deeds shall be apostate." 1 Enoch 93:9

As we shall see we can look back on history now and confirm the fact that the apostasy has indeed happened and continues to happen each day! The church system today is built upon the "apo-stasis" ("away from the foundation") rather than upon "stasis" – the "foundation" laid down by the apostles and prophets. Some sects and denominations claim that the foundation (the Law and the Prophets) is "done away and no longer applies to our life." The church system is the "house built upon the sand."

> "Everyone who hears these words of mine, and does not act upon them, will be like a foolish man, who built his house upon the sand. And the rain descended, and the floods came, and the winds blew, and burst against that house, and it fell. And great was its fall." (Matthew 7:26-27)

The church moved away from the original message, given by the prophets and the apostles (those who were sent to deliver the message), to other counterfeit messages. And instead of being "defenders of that which is true and faithful", the church is the defender of the apostasy! The following prophecy in Revelation applies to the church/Babylonian system:

> Come, I will show you the punishment of the great prostitute, who sits on many waters. With her the kings of the earth committed adultery and the inhabitants of the earth were intoxicated with the wine of her adulteries. Then the angel carried me away in the spirit into a desert. There I saw a woman sitting on a scarlet beast that was covered with blasphemous names and had seven heads and ten horns. The woman was dressed in purple and scarlet, and was glittering with gold, precious stones and pearls. She held a golden cup in her hand, filled with abominable things and the filth of her adulteries. This title was written on her forehead: Mystery, Babylon the Great, The mother of prostitutes and of the abominations of the Earth. I saw that the woman was drunk with the blood of the saints. ... The many waters you saw, where the prostitute sits, are people, multitudes, nations and languages. Revelation 17.

THE SEVEN WEEKS/YEARS WAR

The prophecies of Daniel 9 are not sealed, and most of the events prophesied in Daniel 9 refer to the end of the age in which the apostles lived! In 66 A.D. a revolt broke out in Jerusalem. It was sparked by an act of the Roman Procurator Florus who laid his hands on the temple treasury and took 17 talents. This outraged the Jews who proceeded to insult him by taking up baskets of collections for the "poor, unfortunate Florus." This angered the procurator who dispatched a detachment of soldiers against Jerusalem. They captured Jews at random, bound them in fetters and later crucified them.

This further outraged the Jews, which led to further skirmishes and slaughters. All of these things fanned the flames of the zealots and others who looked upon this as an opportunity to revolt against the Romans. The people, carried away by this zeal, determined not to continue the *sacrifices* to Caesar (taxes). This became an act of open rebellion against Rome, which not only angered the Romans, but also became the cause of civil war among the Jews. It became an internal fight with the zealots against the "Peace party" and one group of zealots against another. The zealots wanted freedom from Roman oppression. The "Peace party" wanted to appease the Romans.

The ruler at that time was Agrippa II, a Jew of the family of Herod. He had a curious interest in religions. In fact, he built a tower in his own house so he could peer down into the temple area to watch the priests. At the time of the rebellion, he was away from Judea in Alexandria. Upon hearing about the revolt, he returned to try to persuade the People to abandon this hopeless revolution but his words did not prosper. Civil war broke out as Agrippa II mustered his forces to try to squelch the outbreak, but they were defeated. They were forced out of the upper city and the rebels set fire to his house.

"Confirming a covenant with the mighty …" "Sacrifices Cease!" Daniel

Agrippa II, forced to take up the side with the "Peace party", made an agreement, a covenant with the Romans to assist in squelching the rebellion. In fulfillment of Daniel's prophecy: "He confirmed a covenant with the mighty".

The Romans, upon hearing about the rebellion, called upon Vespasian to gather the armies to Antioch, and he moved at once south to Galilee. Upon arriving there, he had no difficulty taking the entire northern territory. In most cases it capitulated without any loss of life. The Jews formed armies to move against them, but it was a wasted effort because they were hopelessly outnumbered. The rebellion was pushed southward and focused primarily in Jerusalem. Upon hearing of the death of Nero, Vespasian was disturbed by a possible breakup of the empire, and this distracted him from the Jewish rebellion to the matters of Rome. Eventually, Vespasian went to Alexandria and was proclaimed Emperor of the East. Titus, Vespasian's son, was given command of the Roman armies in Judea, and he moved against Jerusalem. Agrippa II was at his side!

This is our first puzzle piece.
- Agrippa II made a covenant with "the mighty".
- This covenant lasted for 7 years!
- He was the "ruler of the people".
- The "people" were the Jews.

A civil war raged in Jerusalem. Titus surrounded the entire city. He captured any who escaped and crucified them in the sight of the people. It was now a matter of time. The people were not only fighting the Romans; they were in the midst of their own civil war and were under siege. Titus had only to wait until they destroyed themselves. The city was divided among three factions of the Jews – one faction was stationed in the temple area, another in the outer court of the temple, and a third in the city. At one point the civil war became so bitter that one of the warring parties, in spite of the siege, set fire to the stores of grain in the city in order to keep food from the others. All during the civil war, the daily sacrifices continued to be offered. But in the summer of 70 A.D., the daily sacrifices ceased. The civil war waging in Jerusalem created a shortage of manpower. Simply put: no one was left who was qualified to carry out the sacrifices.

"The people of the ruler destroy the city and the sanctuary," Daniel

The prophecy states that the "people of the ruler who would come would destroy the city and the sanctuary".
- They laid their battles lines with the sanctuary and the city.
- The Romans laid the siege around Jerusalem while the Jews fought among themselves.
- Agrippa II, "the ruler", at Titus's side, watched the destruction of his kingdom, his people, the city, and finally the temple.

"The House of Dominion shall be burnt with fire," Enoch

Shortly after the Jews stopped making sacrifices, Titus made an assault on the temple area. He brought in battering rams to make a breach in the wall. The Jews built other walls to keep him out, but to no avail. This was during the summer of 70 A.D. To assist in preventing the Romans from getting into the temple area through the west, the Jews brought flammable material or oil into the temple area and poured it into the western corridors. If any happened to get into those chambers in the wall, they were to be immediately torched and there was no escape. When Titus arrived at the outer court of the temple area, he held a war meeting, in which he gave orders to his generals to not destroy the temple. The Romans now had possession of the outer court and were attempting to quench the other fires set by the Jews.

The very next day, the Jews in the Inner Court area proceeded in two onslaughts to drive the Romans out of the Outer Court. During the skirmish someone picked up a burning timber from one of the fires and hurled it in the direction of the temple. His torch went into the temple and set it on fire! Upon hearing this Titus and his generals came to the temple area and gave orders to quench the fire, but they could not stop the fighting. The Jews, pitching firebrands, succeeded in burning the temple to the ground.

Thus, as prophesied, "the people", the Jews, destroyed the city and the sanctuary, contrary to the wishes of the Romans. The Romans wanted to prevent inflaming another Jewish revolt, created by destroying their temple. Titus also did not want the temple destroyed. But the Jews, because of their own zeal and civil war, succeeded in destroying both the city and the temple! The entire city was razed; not one stone left on another.

This war lasted for 7 years, and was called the "seven years war." It ended in 73 A.D. when the final holdout of the famed Masada was captured.

- Jerusalem was destroyed.
- The Sanhedrin was abolished.
- The priests were out of work.
- The regular sacrifices ceased.
- Only the Pharisees and the Rabbis remained.

THE CITY REBUILT WITH STREETS AND A TRENCH ...

In fulfillment of the prophecy, during the time that followed the war, Jerusalem was "rebuilt" into a Roman camp. This required the building of streets and trenches. Trenches were used for either the control of rainwater, or for the control of human excrement – latrines. Skirmishes continued during the years that followed. These were indeed "troubled times!"

For additional information on this period, I would strongly recommend Josephus' work, *The Wars of the Jews* and Emil Schürer's, *A History of the Jewish People in the time of Jesus*.

This completes the 7 "week" division of the 70 "weeks" or "sevens." The years 66 A.D. to 73 A.D. represent the seven years of the covenant of the "ruler with the mighty." In the midst of this "seven", in 70 A.D., the sacrifices and offerings ended. The Temple was burned with fire. The people, by their rebellion, caused the destruction of the city and the sanctuary.

THE COMING OF THE FALSE MESSIAH

The event that relates to the coming of the "anointed one" is the decree to rebuild and restore Jerusalem. Most Christian seminaries teach that is the decree of Artaxerxes to rebuild the city after which the Jews under the leadership of Ezra returned to build the wall of Jerusalem.

Is the command of Artaxerxes part of the prophecies of Daniel 9?

This has always been a puzzle because of the difficulty of making all of the prophecies of Daniel 9 tie in with any significant event in Jesus' ministry. Tradition argued that the command of Artaxerxes was given in 458 B.C. Then what the commentaries and other prophecy students have mistakenly done is to add 70 weeks times 7 days per week to 458 B.C. and come up with 33 A.D. and declare that this is time Jesus started his ministry.

However, the prophecy states that the period of time from the decree to coming of a "messiah" was seven weeks *and* sixty two weeks and that equals sixty-nine weeks – not seventy!

> "From the issuing of a decree to restore and rebuild Jerusalem until a messiah, the prince [ruler, captain], there will be *seven weeks and sixty-two weeks."*

Assuming that the decree of Artaxerxes is the one mentioned here and assuming that this decree was made in 458 B.C., makes the 7 and 62 weeks or 483 years (69 x 7 days per week) end at 26 A.D. Yes, if you do add another "seven" you arrive at 33 AD. But this does not follow the statements of the prophecy! (Remember, there is no year zero.)

If you were to take all of the English translations of Daniel 9 and compare them you would quickly become confused. The tradition that Daniel 9 foretells the coming of Jesus has forced the translators to stand on their heads to try to make it say what they want. The main problem is due to the fact that the prophecy uses words meaning "anointed prince" or "messiah". And they *assume* this a reference to Jesus. However, as you shall see, this is not the case. Jesus did not apply these prophecies of Daniel to himself! The reason is that they don't apply to Him at all! Instead, they apply to the False Messiah Jesus warned about! You will see that the "anointed prince" of Daniel 9 was a false anointed one, whom Jesus said would come. (Matt. 24:24).

The Seven Years War above referred to the first event of the close of the age, as given by Enoch – the burning of the temple. That was the first seven years or "weeks" of the Daniel 9 prophecy, the time when a covenant was made by the ruler, and when the sacrifices ceased.

Now we come to the *62 week/year* period. At the end of this 62 week or year

period the false messiah was to be cut off, with nothing left.
- Who was this false messiah?
- Who gave the decree to restore and rebuild Jerusalem?
- When was the decree given?
- What was the abomination of desolation that both Jesus and Gabriel spoke about?

We still have some pieces to put into the puzzle. First, let's settle the matter of the decree.

From the time of the end of the "Seven-year war" in 73 A.D. to about 135 A.D., Jerusalem was only a Roman camp. The destruction was so bad that it did not look like it had once been a great city. You read earlier that this fulfills the prophecy of the rebuilding with only streets and trenches. But in 135 A.D. another Roman, Hadrian, known for his fine building programs, set his sights on Jerusalem. He wanted to build a city there that would stand as a monument for Roman worship. Up to this time, the Romans had been extorting offerings from the Jews for the temple of Jupiter in Rome. But now Hadrian dreamed of Aelia Capitolina, on the sight were Jerusalem once stood. In place of the temple would be another temple, this one to Jupiter in support of the worship of Capitoline Jupiter, the official state religion, as well as the only religion to which Hadrian had any affection.

During his visit to Syria *in 130 A.D., Hadrian gave the decree to rebuild and restore Jerusalem* to its former magnificence; only its new magnificence was to be of heathen character. This was a fatal proposal.

Schürer wrote:

> The rearing of magnificent buildings and the founding of cities was the work to which Hadrian devoted the energies of his life. But this proposal must also have been regarded as a blow in the face of Judaism. So long as Jerusalem lay in ruins, the Jews could cherish the hope of its restoration. The founding of a heathen city, the erection of a heathen temple on the holy place, put an end to these hopes in terrible manner. It was an outrage as great as that which Antiochus Epiphanes had formerly committed, and was answered, as that had been, by a general uprising of the excited People.

As long as Hadrian was in the territory, the Jews remained quiet. However, their anger did not cease. In A.D. 132, when Hadrian was not in the neighborhood, they broke out into a revolt. The leader of the revolt was a man named Kokhba or Bar-Kokhba, which means, "Star" or "Son of the Star." The reference to the "Star" indicates how he was considered by the Rabbis and by the People as the "Star of Judah" from Numbers 24:17. He was also known as Simon or Shimeon.

Again Schürer:

> As in the days of Vespasian, so also at this time there was a widespread idea that the day had come when the old prophecy of the prophets would be fulfilled, and Israel would cast off the yoke of the Gentiles.

Coins were minted during the outbreak bearing the inscription, "Simon, Prince of Israel." Other coins show a star over the temple. The fact that a star was associated with him indicated that the Jews regarded him as the Star of Judah, a favorite designation of the Jews for the Messiah! Rabbi Akiba, the most celebrated doctor of the law of his time, announced Simon Bar-Kokhba to be the long awaited Messiah, "This is the King Messiah." Simon Bar-Kokhba is reported to have called himself the Messiah! The Christians wrote that Bar-Kokhba bewitched the Jews by means of miracles and the Christians refused to regard this man as The Messiah. So, this new "Messiah" persecuted them with peculiar violence as Eusebius and Justin Martyr testified.

> "The Jews at that time were under the command of a man name Bar-Kokhba, which means a star -- a bloodthirsty man who on the strength of his name [which implied Messiahship], as if he had slaves to deal with, paraded himself as a luminary come down from heaven to shine upon their misery." Eusebius.

> "In a recent Jewish war, Bar-Kokhba, leader of the Jewish insurrection, ordered the Christians alone to be sentenced to terrible punishments if they did not deny Jesus Christ and blaspheme him." Justin Martyr

Thus, the words of Jesus were fulfilled concerning the terrible persecution that was to come.

THE 69 *LITERAL* WEEKS!

How long was the period between Hadrian's decree to rebuild and restore Jerusalem until the coming of this new "messiah"? The answer lies in a clever twist on the prophecy. Now weeks that were at one time "years" become actual weeks – exactly 7 + 62 calendar weeks! Hadrian gave the decree in 130 A.D. The new leader came on the scene and the revolt broke out in 132 A.D. – *69 literal weeks later!* It is also interesting that the Jews considered this year to be a sabbatical year, and their tradition was that the messiah would come in a sabbatical year. The Romans looked upon this latest revolt with as much seriousness as the rebellion in 66 A.D. The Jewish fighters took up refuge in the mountains, caves, and subterranean passages and terrorized the entire region of Judea with their raids. They even managed to take the Roman Camp on the sight of Jerusalem. Coins were minted that contained, along with the date, the inscriptions, "The First Year of the Freeing of Israel," or "The Second Year of the Freeing of Israel." They also contained the name "Jerusalem."

Again, the Romans were forced to muster their troops and move in strength on Judea. One writer said, "the whole world, so to speak, was in commotion." This time however, Jerusalem was not the focal point of the conflict. Instead, attention had to be directed toward the People.

The end came "like a flood" as the flood of armies swept over Judea. Rebel strongholds became the targets. Thus, the entire area of Judea, including most of its cities and fortresses became involved. The strength of the revolt forced the Romans to kill the rebels, lay siege to many cities, and destroy croplands and livestock. They razed the cities to eliminate hiding places for rebels. But the Romans also paid a heavy price in these conflicts, and Hadrian had to omit from his letters to Rome his usual greeting, "he and the army were well".

The last hiding place of Bar-Kokhba and his followers was the mountain stronghold of Beth-ther. After a long and stubborn defense, this stronghold was conquered. The Romans found Bar-Kokhba, "the originator of all the mad fanaticism which had called down the punishment."

Again Schürer:

> With the fall of Beth-ther the war was brought to a close, after having continued for somewhere about *three and a half years:* A.D. 132-135.

Thus, the revolt ended in 135 A.D. Bar-Kokhba, the false messiah-prince, had nothing left:

- There was not a fighting man left in Judea. Over 580,000 men were killed, not including those who died because of their wounds or from the famine.

- Judea was turned into a desert.
- Fifty fortresses, 985 villages destroyed.
- The number of Jews sold away as slaves was innumerable.
- Many more died of hunger or shipwreck as they were transported to other countries.
- The desolation of the area and the dispersion of the People was complete.

Thus, the prophecy was fulfilled. "After 62 weeks the anointed one [messiah] would be cut off and have nothing." The period from 73 A.D. (the end of the seven years war) to 135 A.D. when the messiah was cut off is 62 years! Now that Judea had been reduced to nothing, the task of rebuilding and restoring Jerusalem was carried out.

- Hadrian rebuilt Jerusalem as the city, Aelia Capitolina.
- He erected a temple to Jupiter on the sight of the former temple. Other gods represented in the city were Bacchus, Serapis, Astarte, and the Dioscuri.
- A temple to Aphrodite (Astarte or Easter) stood on the place where, according to Christian tradition, the sepulchre of Christ had been.
- A statue of Hadrian was put in the new temple.
- He succeeded doing what Antiochus Epiphanes had in vain attempted. For this reason the messenger Gabriel tied the prophecies together.

Although Hadrian rebuilt Jerusalem and placed his own temples and god there, this part of the prophecy is open ended because it speaks of a time in the future:

> "The one who causes desolations (makes desolate) will come on the wings of abominations, *until the desolations that have been decreed are poured out.*"

Other translations say:

> And on the wing of the temple will be the disastrous abomination *until the end, until the doom assigned to the devastator.* (TJB)
>
> And the one who causes desolation will place abominations on a wing of the temple *until the end that is decreed is poured out upon him.* (NIV)

From this time, it was illegal for a Jew to enter the city. And in fact, any Jew in Judea was subject to arrest and sold into slavery. But Jerusalem even today is divided among the gentile nations and the Jews. The regular sacrifices are to this day not offered. There is no temple. And where are the priests?

Jesus' warning was to be heeded, "When you see the abomination of desolation, stand in the holy place, then let those who are in Judea flee to the mountains [other nations]."

Of all the places in the world for the Jews to live, Judea became the most dangerous.
- The people were dispersed.
- Desolations had been decreed and carried out.
- The age was brought to a close.
- The Age of Apostasy began.
- The gentile domination of Israel began.

SIMEON BAR-KOKHBA: SON OF THE STAR

The Chronological Table in the Jerusalem Bible states that in 132 AD Simeon Bar-Koseba seized Jerusalem. He was *acknowledged by Rabbi Akiba as the Messiah* and as the Star (Numbers 24:17). "Bar-Koseba" changed his name to Bar-Kokeba or Bar-Kokhba (Hebrew), which means "Son of a Star". This "Messiah" persecuted the Christians because they refused to join his revolt against the Romans. Bar-Kokhba perished in August of 135 AD, *62 years after the end of the seven years war in 73 AD*. The false messiah prince, Simon Bar-Kokhba, ruled three and one-half years. Although Bar-Kokhba was considered a hero then and even now, the people, because of their blindness, followed a messiah who led them into desolation and dispersion.

Yigael Yadin, author of *Masada*, also wrote the book, *Bar-Kokhba, The rediscovery of the legendary hero of the last Jewish Revolt against Imperial Rome*:

> *Sixty-two years* after the destruction of Jerusalem, a fresh revolt erupted against the Romans, this time in the Holy Land itself. The war of Bar-Kokhba, or the so-called Second Revolt, was a cruel war, perhaps more cruel than the First Revolt. p 18
>
> Talmudic sources also refer quite frequently to what they call Kozbian coins; and indeed the coins of Bar-Kokhba, of which thousands have been found, were the only tangible evidence we had of the Second Revolt. All of Bar-Kokhba's coins

— both silver and bronze — are struck upon Roman coins. ... Many of the coins bear the given name of Bar-Kokhba "Shimeon", sometimes with the additional title, "*Prince [Nasi] of Israel*". p. 26,27

The gathering storm unleashed thunder and lightening [and a flood]. Hadrian mobilized his entire force and put it under the command of his best general, Julius Severus. Bar-Kokhba, in retreat, found himself *short of men* and food. He sent desperate dispatches to the oasis of En-gedi — for a while still remote from the battle-field — requesting provisions and the mobilization of fugitives, but apparently in vain. p. 253

The Jewish Study Bible, in a footnote to Numbers 24:17 says:
Based on this verse, some sages renamed this leader to Bar-Kokhba, "the son of the star" and viewed him as a messianic figure. The revolt was a miserable failure.

The Mystery of the Missing "Week"

So far we have only examined the 7 and 62 week periods of Daniel 9. There are 70 weeks, not just 69. In addition, the prophecy concerns events that will occur at the end of the age. But Jesus covered events for both ages in the Olivet prophecies.

We saw examples of how each "week" can be applied to a year. We know the weeks can be applied to literal weeks as we know them. We have examples showing how a "week" can be a period of seven years. The stopping of the sacrifices happened in the middle of a "week" in the Seven Years war. The false messiah was cut off in the middle of a "week", three and one half years after he began his rebellion.

The use of the Hebrew plural "sevens" שבעים opens the door to apply the same 70 sevens in different ways. In the words of Daniel, "Seventy sevens are to be *cut up or intersected* on your people." Because of this, it is often better to refer to Daniel's "week" as a "period of a seven" which could mean a "year", "seven years", and "seven days," one literal week. The word "seven" was carefully chosen to refer to different time periods as required by the prophecy. Referring back to Enoch's revelation, the sixth week or age ended in 135 A.D. with the dispersion of the people.

We now live in Enoch's seventh week or age. Jesus' prophecy covered the close of two ages: the sixth "week" and the seventh "week" of Enoch's prophecy! Do the 70 weeks of Daniel refer to the close of two ages – the sixth and the seventh or to one age? Sixty-nine of Daniel's 70 weeks close the sixth age. Where to we place the one remaining week? The clue lies in the beginning of the prophecy and reveals the most amazing event of them all! The prophecy states:

> Seventy weeks have been decreed (נֶחְתַּךְ) for your people and your holy city, to finish the transgression, to make an end of sin, to make atonement for iniquity, to bring in everlasting righteousness, to seal up vision and prophecy, and to anoint the most holy [place]. Daniel 9:24 NAS

Not one of these was fulfilled in 66-135 AD (7 + 62 "weeks")! The misapplication of Daniel's 70 weeks to only the "ministry of Jesus" has caused this confusion and blinded People from the truth. Even though the word "messiah" is used often in the Scriptures, it isn't applied to Jesus in every case. King Saul was a messiah. So were David and Solomon. Its general meaning is someone anointed like a King for a special purpose: to lead the people. In the case of Bar-Kokhba, he was a "messiah" who led the People to destruction.

You've seen how Enoch prophesied about the burning of the temple and about the desolation and dispersion of the people. But he also prophesied about another very important event that also happened in the sixth age ...

"In it a man shall ascend!" Enoch

The popular 70 weeks translations contain too much Christian bias. So to clear that out, we must read it again from the Jewish Study Bible:

> Seventy weeks have been decreed [cut up, divided, intersected] for your people and your holy city until the measure of transgression is filled and that of sin complete, until iniquity is expiated, and eternal righteousness ushered in; and prophetic vision ratified and the Holy of Holies anointed.
> Daniel 9:24

As you will see this refers to a time *yet in the future* when another false messiah-king will lead a deceived and apostate *world* into desolations bringing another age to its end.

After that, a new age will dawn upon the world and human kind.

5   The Seventh Age: The Great Apostasy

Enoch prophesied that the seventh age or "week" *to the "time of the establishment of the righteous kingdom,"* would be a time of apostasy, with many works, but all works would be apostate!

Apostasy means "building without a good foundation." Jesus referred to it as "building your house upon the sand" as opposed to "building your house upon a rock foundation." When the storm comes, you can guess which one will not make it. From Enoch's point of view, it means we must build on that which *he* knows is solid. After all, Enoch received revealed knowledge. And Elahim "translated him so that he would not see death." Scripture says Enoch did not die! Elahim took him from the earth and gave him a place in the Domain of Elahim .

Some claim the apostasy happens only at the "end of the world," whatever that means. The age of apostasy of Enoch's vision characterizes the events of an age, covering many centuries during which deception and lies thrive and rule over the world.

How Apostasy Starts

Apostasy starts by building a religion not based upon the truth, but upon rites, practices, and dogma. Doctrines and religious practices that started thousands of years ago, during the time of Nimrod, continue to color and influence religion to our time. The leaders of a religion find ways to convince the people that to "save their souls" they should only follow the leaders' teachings. The leaders also coerce people to submit themselves to the leaders' or overseers' way or face dire consequences. It is a power play for the control of your life!

These leaders craft an intricate program of rituals and liturgy including images, special clothing, required meetings, forms of services, holidays, special vocabulary, and veneration of their own history. They often cater to the fears and poverty of the masses and promise that if the masses will do this or that, it will go well for them. And if the people submit to practices like "confession" and "baptism," they can be assured of "escaping hell" and "achieving heaven." Rather than helping people find the way to freedom, knowledge and strength, apostasy with its many religions leads to slavery, fear, and ignorance.

Deception: The Hallmark of Apostasy

Jesus spoke of the coming great deception in the Olivet prophecies when he said many would come using his name, saying that He was the Christ and would succeed at deceiving the masses! John saw the great deception as the opening of the First Seal and recorded it in the book of Revelation. He saw a white horse, with one sitting on it wearing a crown, holding a bow. He went out as a conqueror bent on conquest! Some say this is a vision of Jesus. Instead the horseman symbolizes what Jesus warned about:

> "A multitude will come in my name, proclaiming that I am the Christ, and will deceive *the masses.*"

The conquering rider on a white horse characterizes the Age of Apostasy with its powerful deceptions. Compare this with Revelation 19. Here another rides a white horse, but he is not a deceiver:

* This One has many crowns on His head.
* He makes war and judges with justice.
* He wields a sharp sword.
* His name is the "Word of God".
* The two images look alike. But the first conquers the people by deception.
* The second conquers deception by Truth.
* His name is "Faithful and True".

The Paul Problem

Starting from the middle of the second century CE very powerful religious organizations rose up and conquered the minds of the people. When I was a young Christian, I used to read Paul almost exclusively to the rest of the Bible. But I wondered why Paul never quoted Jesus or referred to Jesus's teachings in his letters. Later, as I began my post-graduate work, I studied the Law, the Prophets and the Writings of the Old Testament and the Hebrew Scriptures.

The Good News that the Apostles preached is in those books not is Paul's letters.

There are many critics of Paul and his theology – too many to list in this book. But I must include a few. So that you don't think I alone am being cynical about Paul.

Albert Schweitzer, theologian and philosopher, in his writing showed that even though Paul's writing contained a Christ-mysticism relationship, it did not show the "God-mysticism" that the Apostles preached. "In Paul there is no God-mysticism." Here are some of Dr. Schweitzer's statements regarding the Paul problem:

> Critics demanded of theology proof that the canonical Paul and his Epistles belonged the early Christianity; and the demand was justified.
>
> The rapid diffusion of Paul's ideas can be attributed to his belief in the death of Christ signified the end of the [Mosaic] Law. In the course of one or two generations this concept became the common property of the Christian faith, *although it stood in contradiction to the tradition teaching represented by the Apostles at Jerusalem.*
>
> What is the significance for our faith and for our religious life, of the fact that the Gospel of Paul is different from the Gospel of Jesus? ... The attitude which Paul himself takes up towards the Gospel of Jesus is that he does not repeat it in the words of Jesus, and does not appeal to its authority. ...
>
> The fateful thing is that the Greek, the Catholic, and the Protestant theologies all contain the Gospel of Paul in a form that does not continue the Gospel of Jesus, *but displaces it.*

There is one statement made by Paul, rarely heard by Christians, that actually supports Jesus' statement that He came to fulfill the Law and not do away with it. Peter said that Paul's writing were hard to understand. The following passage illustrates that:

> For all have sinned and fall short of the glory of God, being justified as a gift by His grace through the redemption, which is in Christ Jesus; whom God displayed publicly as a propitiation in his blood through faith.

Paul wrote in Greek, but all those multi-syllable words came from the Latin

Vulgate making this even harder to understand. "Justified" means "declared not guilty." "Redemption" means to "pay a debt." "Propitiation" is "a sacrifice or payment required to regain the good will of someone." And "faith" means "being true your promises." But the key verse follows (from two translations):

> This was to demonstrate His righteousness, because in the forbearance [patience] of God he passed over the sins previously committed! [NAS]

> He did this to demonstrate His justice, because in His forbearance *he had left the sins committed beforehand unpunished.* [NIV]

These are not just any old sins. Paul had to be talking about the sins as defined by the Law and confirmed by a covenant. In the verses that immediately follow, Paul explains that the character trait of "faith" possessed by God required the fulfillment of the Law and this sacrifice actually caused the Law to be applicable not only to the Eyahudim but also the rest of the world! Also it is not the Latin "faith" or "fides" or "belief" that makes this work for everyone. It does not depend upon whether or not we believe, understand, or even hear about it. This *pistis* (Greek) "faith" is a quality of character of Elahim and Eyahuwah to keep their word and make the sacrifice work for all humanity dead, living, or yet to be born! Eyahuwah, covenanted with Israel that if they kept the Law they would have Life, if not then they would die. They agreed to this life or death covenant not only for themselves but also for the descendants. They agreed to the Law and promised to keep it, and if they didn't, they agreed to receive death, sickness, and captivity. They didn't keep their part of the contract. So Eyahuwah exercised patience and passed over the accrued punishments and came in the flesh to live with the people. He then made the payment of their debt and thereby purchased not only the people of all the tribes of Israel but also all the people of the world.

This is the Good News, the Gospel that was not preached.

Until now.

Although, this is the meaning of these words from Roman 3, Peter is right, they are hard to understand and unstable men twisted them to mean something else. The job of this Covenant Maker was to keep the contract, even if he had to be born of the flesh and become one of the People to pay their debt himself, though he did not owe anything. He, with diligence, kept the Law as written and intended. He had nothing to do with the Babylonian Talmud, which the Pharisees used to restate the Law in their words. They accused him of breaking *their* law.

Malachi, a post-exilic prophet, saw the change that had taken place in the people during exile as Babylonian captives. In place of the Law, the people followed the supposed "oral" teaching now written down by the sect of the Pharisees in the Babylonian Talmud. They adopted the Babylonian calendar on which they placed their feast days and Sabbaths. Malachi wrote:

> But you profane it [My Name] by saying of the Lord's table, "It is defiled", and of its food, "It is contemptible." And you say, "What a burden," and you sniff at it contemptuously.
> v1:12

Paul taught some good things, but he also taught things contrary to what the apostles and disciples taught. Paul created a religious structure based upon overseers, otherwise known as Baals. He taught the overseers to rule over the people as the leaders of nations do. Paul designed a structure similar to Roman rule and set out to proselytize people to follow him. In Paul's description of the requirements of an overseer (I Timothy), he never mentions that the overseer must be a servant. Paul taught that he must be capable of ruling. This he emphasizes when he wrote that the elders who "ruled well" should be given double pay.

Erich Fromm, in *The Dogma of Christ* wrote:

> This *had been* the religion of a community of equal brothers, *without hierarchy or bureaucracy*, [but] was converted into 'the Church', the reflected image of the absolute monarchy of the Roman Empire.

Jesus taught the disciples to NOT follow the way of the nations. Instead they were to become *servants and helpers*. Whenever the disciples tried to determine who was to be the greatest among them, he rebuked them, and said the greatest of all would be the one who was the servant of all, not an "overseer."

Peter wrote that Paul's letters were hard to understand and he addressed Paul as "our beloved brother", not as an apostle. Paul's writings were used by the unstable and deceivers to twist the meaning and use it for their own gain and power. In his entire second letter Peter wrote about the problem of false teachers among the People. He told them that the apostles did not follow "cleverly devised tales."

He urged the People to follow the prophets of the Hebrew Scriptures because the Prophets were men set apart by God. They did not speak according to the desires or will of men, but rather by the Holy Spirit.

Peter warned about men who would secretly introduce destructive heresies. He said they exploit people with false words and revel in their deceptions. Peter specifically states that his second letter reminds the people *to remember the words of the Prophets, and the commandments of the Lord and Savior as taught by the Apostles.*

Here is how deceivers poison people. They cause them to drink a mixture containing both the poison and something that tastes good. By mixing a fatal amount of error with enough truth to make one think they are doing right, many have been deceived and led into apostasy.

In an apostate condition there is much talk about Jesus, even saying that he is the Christ, singing about him, preaching about him, while at the same time being committed to what is really deception and false knowledge.

Following apostate teachers resulted in the dark ages, ignorance, intolerance, inquisitions, murders, and misapplied prophecies!

The age of apostasy took hold in the second century CE and continues to this day. But the seed was sown in the first century.

Jesus said the Spirit of Truth "will guide you into all truth and show you things to come". But when truth becomes compromised among those who are weak and those who do not have the Spirit of Truth, such compromise "quenches" the Spirit of Truth and opens the door to deceptions and lies of the apostasy.

The writings of Paul in the New Testament contain things that cause confusion and trouble for disciples today, even as they did in the first century.

Paul held that the problems were with the Apostles and congregations at Jerusalem, but the apostles there had serious problems with Paul and his followers.

Jesus's and Apostles' teachings came from the Hebrew Scriptures, from Moses and the Prophets, which some people think were done away, mainly because of twisted statements in Paul's letters.

If Hebrew Scriptures and the teachings of the Apostles cannot corroborate Paul's letters then those letters must be questioned and carefully examined by those who have the Spirit of Truth.

The true touchstone is the Law and the Prophets.

To their own hurt many take Paul's writings as authority to declare the Hebrew Scriptures null and void. This is upside down and backward. This is the seed that produced the apostate generation prophesied by Enoch. Apostasy is the main characteristic of the seventh age — the age in which we live!

Peter wrapped up his powerful second letter warnings with these words:

> But according to His promise we are looking for a new heavens and a new earth, in which righteousness dwells. [A quote from Enoch.]
>
> Therefore, beloved, since you look for these things, be diligent to be found by Him in peace, spotless and blameless, and regard the patience of our Lord salvation.
>
> Just as also our beloved brother Paul, according to the wisdom given him, wrote to you, as also in all his letters, speaking in them of these things, among which are some things hard to understand, which the untaught and unstable distort, as they do also the rest of the Scriptures, to their own destruction.
>
> You therefore, beloved, knowing this beforehand, be on guard lest, being carried away by the error of unprincipled men, you fall from your own steadfastness, but grow in the grace and knowledge of our Lord and Savior Jesus Christ*. 2 Peter 3:13-18

This was Peter's polite way of giving the People a "heads up" regarding the letters of Paul and the trouble they will bring. You can scan the letters of Paul and not come across the "knowledge of our Lord and Savior." Instead you find Paul's "knowledge" and what he thought *about* Jesus and his version of another gospel.

In one of Paul's many complaints he admitted:

> "Even though I may not be an apostle to others ['the Apostles and the Lord's brothers and Cephas (Peter)'], surely I am to you [his followers]." 1 Corinthians. 9:2,5

Peter clearly did not grant him the title "apostle" and then went on to explain how dangerous Paul's letters were and what threat they held for the disciples. By saving this for the end of his letter, Peter clearly set the stage to reemphasize the deception and false teaching Paul brought into the early church.

Even though Paul claimed he had a vision that the witnesses neither saw or heard, the words that Paul said "that Jesus told him" were quotes out of Greek writings! It seams as though Paul's epiphany revealed to him a different way to destroy the people. Peter used the example of Balaam to illustrate the situation. Balaam caused the People of Israel to fall under a curse by deceiving the people to follow *his* way and thereby bring the curse upon them. Paul, on his way to persecute the disciples, had a new idea! Rather than persecuting them, he decided to infiltrate the group and teach the disciples to follow a "better way" and "new gospel." Paul set up a church body and structures designed to rule over the People and make the People fall in the same way that the People of Israel fell by following Balaam's way.

The church is clearly "Pauline". The dogma and structure of the church and its teachings is based upon Paul's letters and not upon the teachings of Jesus. Often it sounds like the church considers anything outside of Paul's letters as "add color" material and nice sounding stories. Many churches even today continue to teach that the Law is "done away." The church introduced and upholds holidays that were part of Baalism including the worship of Astarte or Ishtar, the birth of Tammuz in December, and the resurrection of Chronos or Saturn, the Sun God, who arises from the dead on the morning of the spring equinox, or now on "Ishtar" Sunday morning.

Paul stated his qualifications, among other things, that he was "in regard to the Law, a Pharisee." He used this "qualification" when he rebuked Peter:

> You are a Jew, yet you live like a gentile and not like a Jew.
> How is it then, that you force gentiles to follow Jewish customs? Galatians 2:14

Spoken by a true Pharisee. The Law is not a "Jewish custom." The Pharisees made an icon of the Law and replaced it with their preferred "customs" including such things as making it unlawful to tie or untie more than two knots on the Sabbath. It was like saying Peter was wrong because he sat down with gentiles.

I found, after "fasting" from Paul for several years and learning the Gospel from the Hebrew Scriptures and other important documents like the Book of Enoch, that Paul now read like someone who tossed vocabulary around as though it meant something when it didn't. He was bitter, domineering, deceitful, and a self-appointed apostle. He also made others apostles who were loyal to him.

Jesus told the People, "by their fruits, you shall know them." If Paul's followers were the fruit of his labors, then his tree produced, among other things, incest, fornication, adultery, theft, unfaithfulness, hatred, murder, envy, strife, and lawlessness. Rather than being disciples like Jesus' disciples, these were those who liked to go to meetings and be seen together. They followed the ways of the Pharisees. Paul was a highly trained Pharisee! Reading between the lines of Paul's letters reveals a picture of trouble in all the churches started and managed by him. Jealousy in Rome. Fornication in Thessalonica. Incest, drunkenness, and adultery in Corinth. Boastfulness in Galatia. The list goes on and reflects the conditions in churches to this day.

The conclusion:
* The Apostles preached a message that did NOT depend upon the teachings of Paul.
* The Apostles were NOT followers of Paul. Nor did Paul follow either the teachings of Jesus or the Apostles.
* The Apostles, appointed by Jesus, did not preach or teach Paul's doctrines.
* The Gospel can be understood in clarity through the Scriptures without Paul.

The new discoveries of the past few years, the Gospels of Thomas, Philip, and Truth, reveal a completely different picture of the teachings of the Apostles. Scholars considers these as *anti-Gnostic* writings that differ greatly from the Gnostic material found at the same time near Nag Hammadi in Egypt. In answer to the question, "Are the Coptic Gospels Gnostic?", Paterson Brown states in *Metalogos: The Gospels of Thomas, Philip, and Truth*:

> While there may well be Gnostic writings amongst the several dozen titles found so significantly near the site of Saint Pachomius archetypal monastery, the three Coptic Gospels in that collection are demonstrably not Gnostic in content. ...
>
> No text, which affirms the basic reality and sanctity of incarnate life [normal life in the flesh], can properly be labeled 'Gnostic'.
>
> The Coptic Gospels of Thomas, Philip, and Truth (like the entire Old Testament, the New Testament Gospels and Acts) explicitly assert the sacred reality of incarnate life. Therefore, they are not Gnostic writings.

My research of these Gospels, including earlier translations, first proved inconclusive. The translations were generally dry. They read as though the scholars did not understand the text they translated. But when I found these, a light came on. These Gospels required spiritual discernment, rather than scholarly analysis. When read in the Spirit, they were as alive as the other Scriptures. Gnostic writings do not have this Spiritual connection. These Gospels showed the Apostles as men of deep spiritual power and understanding. These Gospels revealed that the disciples were far wiser than many would dare to think. If Jesus had a choice between the Law and the Prophets, and Paul's epistles, which would he choose?

> Now that same day two of them were going to a village called Emmaus, about seven miles from Jerusalem. They were talking with each other about everything that had happened. As they talked and discussed these things with each other, Jesus himself came up and walked along with them; but they were kept from recognizing him.
>
> He asked them, "What are you discussing together as you walk along?"
>
> They stood still, their faces downcast. One of them, named Cleopas, asked him, "Are you only a visitor to Jerusalem and do not know the things that have happened there in these days?"
>
> "What things?" he asked.
>
> "About Jesus of Nazareth," they replied. "He was a prophet, powerful in word and deed before God and all the People. The chief priests and our rulers handed him over to be sentenced to death, and they crucified him; but we had hoped that he was the one who was going to redeem Israel. And what is more, it is the third day since all this took place. In addition, some of our women amazed us. They went to the tomb early this morning but didn't find his body. They came and told us that they had seen a vision of angels, who said he was alive. Then some of our companions went to the tomb and found it just as the women had said, but him they did not see."
>
> He said to them, "How foolish you are, and *how slow of heart to believe all that the prophets have spoken*! Did not the

Christ have to suffer these things and then enter his glory?" *And beginning with Moses and all the Prophets,* he explained to them what was said *in all the Scriptures* concerning himself.

As they approached the village to which they were going, Jesus acted as if he were going farther. But they urged him strongly, "Stay with us, for it is nearly evening; the day is almost over." So he went in to stay with them.

When he was at the table with them, he took bread, gave thanks, broke it and began to give it to them. Then their eyes were opened and they recognized him, and he disappeared from their sight. They asked each other, "Were not our hearts burning within us while he talked with us on the road and opened the Scriptures to us?"

They got up and returned at once to Jerusalem. There they found the Eleven and those with them, assembled together and saying, "It is true! The Lord has risen and has appeared to Simon." Then the two told what had happened on the way, and how Jesus was recognized by them when he broke the bread. Luke 24:13-35 NIV

Living in an age marked by apostasy presents great challenges. The deception Jesus foretold was to be so great the even the very elect would be deceived. The only way to overcome is to keep our hearts and minds open to the truth.

Eyahushuah said, "Do not think that I came to abolish the Law or the Prophets. I did not come to abolish, but to fulfill. For truly I say to you, *until heaven and earth pass away, not the smallest letter or stroke shall pass away from the Law, until all is accomplished.* Whoever then annuls one of the least of these commandments, and so teaches others, shall be called the least in the kingdom of heaven. But whoever keeps and teaches others, he shall be called great in the kingdom of heaven. For I say to you, that unless your righteousness surpasses that of the scribes and Pharisees, you shall not enter the kingdom of heaven." Matthew 5:17-20

A fountain of truth and wisdom was prepared for us from the beginning, before the heavens and the earth were created:

> And in that place I saw the fountain of righteousness, which was inexhaustible. And around it were many fountains of wisdom. All the thirsty drank of them and were filled with wisdom. And their dwelling place was with the righteous and the holy and the elect. From 1 Enoch 48

> If any of you lacks wisdom, he should ask God, who gives generously to all without finding fault, and it will be given to him. But when he asks, he must believe and not doubt, because he who doubts is like a wave of the sea, blown and tossed by the wind. That man should not think that he will receive anything from *Eyahuwah*; he is a double-minded man, unstable in all he does. James 1:6-7

We need to get back to building on the foundation created before the world began, and stop building our houses on the sand of falsehood and apostasy. We must not allow the great apostasies of our age keep us from the knowledge we need.

Take a moment and make this prayer your own:

Father in heaven. Give me the wisdom and the desire to know and understand the knowledge that leads to eternal life. Clear my head and cleanse my heart from the lies of apostasy and help me comprehend the glorious Truth. Grant me the gift of your Holy Spirit, who, as my Mother, will guide me into all truth. I know that You can do this for me, and I know that You will. I will wait and watch for your answer. Thank you for this great gift.

6 Feasts, High Days, and the Revealed Calendar

The Feasts and High Days come from the Law or *Torah* in Hebrew. They were part of the Covenant made between Eyahuwah and the people. The history of the people shows that on these days special events happened that forever changed their lives. As we shall see, this will continue.

Theologically, it makes sense to consider that Jesus would have followed *Enoch's* calendar, and that his ministry, from Passover to Passover, according to John's record, aligned with this calendar at that time. Even though there are 1.242 more days in the year, Enoch's calendar starts on the spring equinox each year. It differs from the 360-day Egyptian Calendar only in the placing of the extra days. The Egyptians placed five days at the end of the 360-day year. Enoch's calendar places one day at the end of each quarter. The extra time that we gained after the flood now has to be placed at the end of the year. This day would not be considered a day in the week. Instead, it would be a period of time with no name between the third and fourth days of the week. It is a cursed time.

Following the Laws of the calendar, there are no leap years in Enoch's calendar because the extra time is absorbed by the "noname" day. The calendar officially begins on the day of the spring equinox on the fourth day of the week. Thus the reason we need an adjustment at the end of the twelfth months is to allow the earth to catch up with the calendar. We must wait for the equinox in both the spring and the fall and not count the spurious day – even as a weekday! As far and Enoch's calendar is concerned, that extra time does not exist!

Before the church and the Pharisees changed the calendar, the calendar started and ended each year with the spring equinox. And some countries continued to follow that practice until the 18th century.

Earlier we learned that the enormous weather change of the great flood caused the earth to spin faster and increased the number of days from spring equinox to spring equinox. So to keep in sync with the equinoxes the Law placed the Feast and Holy Days in the first and the seventh months of each year. The third month also contains a very important Feast and High Day that we will examine later. The Law, which came after the flood, took into account the difference in the number of days in a year. But the length of the day after the flood differed from the day of Enoch's age by five minutes per day! Enoch's day was longer and this change to a shorter day is not noticeable.

By using the equinoxes as starting points, the feasts line up with the days of the week and with the rest of the year. Although no one can tell the 5 minutes difference in each day at the start of the year in the first month and the start of the seventh month, the difference accumulates. After six months the difference amounts to almost 15 hours. But this is easily corrected by adding an extra day at the end of the year. It would not be a day of the week. At the end of the year, there would be the normal third day of the week, then odd "unlucky" day or cursed day, and then the year begins at the spring equinox on the fourth day of the week.

As far as the extra 1.242 days in the year, it does not need to be considered when determining the Feasts and Holy Days because they are fixed to the equinoxes on the first days of the first and seventh months. The extra time serves as a reminder to Mankind about the "first end" and the great destruction that came upon earth as a consequence of human failure.

We err if we conclude that we cannot follow Enoch's calendar today and know exactly when the feasts, holy days and Sabbath days occur. Though the number of days in a year increased, the equinoxes remained the same. These two solar events form the foundation of the structure of the revealed calendar and make it possible for us to restore it and follow it, if we have the strength and courage to do so.

Here are the references in the Book of Enoch regarding the days marked by solar events:

Verses in Enoch 1, Chapter 72:
* The cycle of the year and months and seasons
* Verse 6,7: The first month and the start of the cycle
* Verse 14: The Summer Solstice (SS)
* Verse 20: The autumnal or Fall Equinox (FE)

* Verse 26: The Winter Solstice (WS)
* Verse 31,32: End of the 12th month, the year completed in 364 days [then], the Spring Equinox (SE) ends the year and begins the next year.

We follow a different calendar because the church aligned with the Romans and "changed the times and the seasons" to suit their own purposes. As a result of the Romans and the church we have a twelfth month called "December" and "Decem" means "tenth!" The Hebrew Scriptures and the Law give no instructions about the Jewish calendar because it is the Babylonian calendar.

Service Schedule for Priests Assigned to 364-day Year

During the first century CE, the priests followed their courses as established by King David centuries earlier. David divided the priests into 24 groups and appointed them by lot to serve in the temple in semi-monthly periods. Each course served two consecutive Sabbaths. The course started on the first and fifteenth day of each month. David's set up the 24 courses based upon a calendar with the twelve 30 day months — the revealed calendar.

The father of John the Baptist served during the course of Abijah. The drawing of the lot assigned Abijah to the last half of the fourth month.

From the discoveries of the Dead Sea Scroll, the Essenes at Qumran kept both the Jewish calendar and Enoch's calendar. John spoke and baptized only a short distance from the settlement there. Both Jesus and John knew what was going on at Qumran. Many believe that both visited and studied there. The disciples in Judea and the Essenes at Qumran fled just prior to the destruction of the Temple. But first, they hid the documents

The Placement of the Feasts and High Days

There are seven Feasts and seven High Days, according to the Law. We do not need to refer to their position on the Jewish calendar because it is a lunar calendar. The Book of Jubilees made it clear that the moon has nothing to do with the times and the seasons as related to the observance of the Feasts and High Days. Only the sun and the solar events (equinoxes and solstices) determine the seasons, the "new year," and the days of the Feasts and High Days.

Each month has 30 days according to the Law of the Calendar. An intercalary day marks the end of each quarter. Each quarter has 13 weeks. Each year has 12 months. The year has exactly 52 weeks and it always starts on the same day of the week. When counting days between calendar events, the intercalary days are not included.

So, even though the Enoch's year has 364 days and our year has 365.242 days, when counting the year you count 360 days and skip the intercalary days. This holds true today. Even though now there are more than 365 days between equinoxes, you still only count 360 days in the year and ignore the intercalary days and any other days or pieces of a day. That is according to Enoch's revelation and the Law of the Calendar. On Enoch's calendar, Feasts and High or Holy Days, fall on the same date and same day of the week each year, because the year always starts on the fourth or middle day of the week.

THE HOLY YEAR, QUARTER 1, ACCORDING TO SCRIPTURE

FIRST MONTH

			1 EQ	2	3	4
5	6	7	8	9	10	11
12	13	14 PS	15 UB	16	17	18
19 WS	20	21 HD	22	23	24	25
26 W1	27	28	29	30		

SECOND MONTH

					1	2
3 W2	4	5	6	7	8	9
10 W3	11	12	13	14	15	16
17 W4	18	29	20	21	22	23
24 W5	25	26	27	28	29	30

THIRD MONTH

1 W6	2	3	4	5	6	7
8 W7	9	10	11	12	13	14
15 FF	16	17	18	19	20	21
22	23	24	25	26	27	28
29	30	31				

Keys to the First Quarter of the Calendar
EQ: Spring Equinox. Year Starts
PS: Passover
UB: Start of Feast of Unleavened Bread; High Day
WS: Wave Sheaf Offering
HD: High Day at the end of the Feast
W1 - W7: Seven Complete Weeks
FF: Feast of Firstfruits/Feast of Weeks. Wave Loaves Offered

Feasts and High Days of the First Month
The first day of the first month is "new year's day" and the spring equinox signals to the People that a new year started. The year has seven feasts and seven High or Holy days. No work is done on a "high" day. High days are also called holy days. The word "holy" means "set apart" from all other days. When kept on the Revealed Calendar, these days are called "clean" days.

The Passover Feast
Passover is not a high day. I repeat: the Passover is not a Sabbath day! Nor is it the first day of the month or year! And contrary to popular opinion, it is not on the 15th day of the month. It falls on the 14th day of the first month starting at sunset. This is always the third day of the week.

When the descendants of Jacob, who is also named Israel, were slaves in Egypt, Moses came and helped free them from their bondage. On the night of the Passover, Moses commanded the People to slay and eat a Lamb.

> Now the Eyahuwah said to Moses and Aaron in the land of Egypt:
>
> "*This month shall be the beginning of months for you. It is to be the first month of the year for you.* Speak to all the congregation of Israel, saying, '*On the tenth of this month* they are each one to take a lamb for themselves, according to their fathers' household, a lamb for each household. Now if the household is too small for a lamb, then he and his neighbor nearest to his house are to take one according to the number of persons in them, according to what he man should eat, you are to divide the lamb.
>
> 'Your lamb should be an unblemished male a year old.

You make take it from the sheep or the goats.

'And you shall keep it *until the fourteenth day of the month*. Then the whole assembly of the congregation of Israel is to kill it at twilight [sunset]. Moreover, they shall take some of the blood and put it on the two door posts and on the lintel of the house in which they eat it. And they shall eat the flesh that same night, roasted with fire, and they shall eat it with unleavened bread and bitter herbs. Do not eat any of it raw or boiled at all with water, but rather roasted with fire, both its head and its legs along with its entrails. And you shall not leave any of it over until the morning, but whatever is [might be] left of it until morning, you shall burn with fire. Now you will eat it in this manner: with your loins girded, your sandals on your feet, and your staff in your hand, and you shall eat it in haste – it is Eyahuwah's Passover. For I will go through the land of Egypt on that night, and will strike down all of the firstborn in the land of Egypt, both man and beast, and against all the gods of Egypt I will execute judgments – I am Eyahuwah. And the blood shall be a sign for you on the houses where you live, and when I see the blood I will pass over you, and no plague will befall you to destroy you when I strike the land of Egypt.

'Now this day will be a memorial to you and you shall celebrate it as a feast to Eyahuwah, *throughout all your generations you are to celebrate it as a permanent ordinance.*'" Exodus 12:1-14 NAS.

The reason behind so much detail as to how to keep the Passover lies in the importance of preserving the symbolism. Keeping the day is one thing, but remembering the symbolism, the images of that day, is equally important.

The coming "out of Egypt" is a powerful image, because Egypt is an image of the deception and bondage of this world. Israel, from the known People of Judah to the unknown "lost tribes", is under bondage and slavery to the power of this world. Trouble, including severe plagues, is destined to come upon the whole world at the end of the seventh age. Any who are part of the world and part of its religions can receive the plagues, wars, and captivity. But if we come out of the world and "touch not the unclean" and come under the protection of the Passover, we can escape these things.

As long as we cling to the world's ways, including its religions, we will not be under the Passover protection and will suffer the same fate as the rest of the world. Some say the Law is "done away" and we don't need to pay any attention to it any more. The Passover is a permanent ordinance. But how can we keep this feast if we don't even know when its day comes?

THE FEAST OF UNLEAVENED BREAD

This Feast starts on the 15th day at sunset. This is a high and holy day, a Sabbath day. It always falls on the *fourth day of the week*. This feast continues for seven days. This is mistakenly called Passover!

On the first day of the week during the Feast of Unleavened Bread, the high priest offers the Wave Sheaf. The Wave Sheaf is a handful of freshly picked wheat and represents the Firstfruit of the harvest. Jesus [Eyahushuah] was a Son of Man and was the *first* "begotten" or conceived by God. He became the Firstborn Son of God by the resurrection from the dead.

The 21st day of the first months is last day of the Feast of Unleavened Bread and always falls on the third day of the week. This is a high and holy day in which no work is to be done.

The images of this feast reveal more about our spiritual life. Bread is an image of spiritual food. But during this Feast we must eat bread made without yeast. It represents spiritual food, uncontaminated by the dogmas and traditions of the religions of the nations. In this case, their former homeland was Egypt. But they are no longer citizens of "Egypt." The events of Passover made their deliverance certain.

The first thing the people of Israel did when they came out of Egypt was to begin a new and pure life, at least symbolically. The image of eating unleavened bread represents that during our Life we must feast on the true bread that comes from heaven. Leaven is an image of impurity, uncleanness and wrongdoing. When bread is "leavened", the leaven "corrupts" the whole loaf. Leaven cannot be removed once it has been added into the bread dough.

But unleavened bread is pure from leaven from the beginning. So we should very careful to feast only on pure spiritual food and that will require abandoning religious traditions and staying free from religious mind control.

The Feast and High Day of the Third Month

The Feast of Weeks is also called Feast of Firstfruits and Pentecost. This feast ties directly to the Feasts, Sabbaths and High days of the first month. All other feasts are fixed to either the first or seventh months. This is the only feast in the Law that comes in the third month.

Beginning with the first full week after the Sabbath that comes *after* the *Wave Sheaf* is offered, seven complete weeks are counted. This fixes the Feast with the events of the first month and, specifically, with the Wave Sheaf offering.

> From the day after the Sabbath [that comes after] the day you brought the sheaf of the Wave Offering, count off seven full weeks. Lev. 23:15

After the completion of seven full weeks, the very next day is the Feast of Weeks and Firstfruits. This is a High day and a double festival and no work is to be done. It is always on the 15th day of the third month and is always on the first day of the week and is the 75th day of the year.

The images of the Feast of Firstfruits and Feast of Weeks have great importance. On this day the *Wave Loaves* are presented before God as an offering. The people make two identical loaves with fine flour mixed with leaven. They make *one* batch of dough and *divide it into two loaves* before baking. The Law says they must do this "in the place where they live." As we shall see, this image of the two Wave Loaves is very powerful

Also as an image of Enoch's vision of the Weeks, the Feast of Weeks falls on the 15th day of the 3rd month after seven full weeks passed. Not only does this feast mark the completion of the seven full weeks, it also is an image of the beginning of the eighth week and the events that follow soon afterward. The Feast of Firstfruits reveals significant prophetic events regarding the Firstfruits.

The combination of feasts and the Wave Loaves offering on a single day make this feast one of the most important of the year!

Several important events happened on this day. The People received the Law and made a covenant with Eyahuwah Elahim on this day. The apostles and disciples received a new covenant written in their hearts by the Holy Spirit. On this day, these Sons of Man, like Jesus [Eyahushuah] before them, were "begotten" by their Father and their Elahim and became the fetal Sons of Elah.

They now lived in the womb of their Mother, the Holy Spirit.

JESUS' DEATH AND THE PASSOVER

Eyahushuah's crucifixion happened according to the Feasts of the revealed calendar.

Remember: from the beginning, days were determined from sunset to sunset not from midnight to midnight. Passover starts at sunset and ends at sunset.

Jesus was taken on Passover, after the supper, in the late evening, after sunset. On Enoch's calendar, this would have been the evening of the 14th day of the first month. This is the third day of the week. After a night of trials, beatings and questioning, they crucified him *on the following morning of Passover day and* He died in the afternoon.

Sunset, marks the end of Passover and the beginning of the Days of Unleavened Bread. On the calendar this begins the fourth or middle day of the week and the 15th day of the month. This day is a Holy or High Day in which no work was done. So Eyahushuah had to be buried *before sunset* — before Passover ended and before the High Day of the Feast of Unleavened bread started. Joseph of Arimathea, Mary's uncle, went to the officials and asked for the body and placed it in his own tomb before sunset.

Three days and three nights from the time on Passover when Eyahushuah was placed in the tomb takes us to the time just before sunset at the end of the *weekly* Sabbath. This means that he would have been resurrected, not on Sunday morning, but before sunset of the weekly Sabbath. Therefore, Mary and the women hurried to the tomb in the evening immediately after the end of the Sabbath to finish the burial process. When they arrived they found the stone rolled back and the tomb empty. A messenger from Elahim met them and asked, "Why do you seek the living among the dead?"

The other women left Mary Magdalene alone in the garden tomb. It was then that Eyahushuah appeared to Mary - on the first day of the week after sunset. "Very early on the first day of the week," is not sunrise or after midnight but rather shortly after the sunset that signaled the end of the weekly Sabbath. Either Eyahushuah was in the tomb for three days and three nights, as he said, or those who teach otherwise call him a liar.

Good Friday and Easter Sunday are inventions of apostate religions and have no place in prophecy. They are traditions that have no foundation in the Scriptures, as is so plainly evident to those who studied Scripture. Obviously, these inventions cannot account for the three days and three nights Eyahushuah spoke about concerning his death and resurrection. Later, we will learn more about the Passover and the Feast of Unleavened Bread that is yet in our future.

The Feasts & High Days of the Seventh Month

The Feast of Trumpets starts on the first day of the seventh month at evening. This is a High day and also the fall equinox and the fourth day of the week. This is NOT the "last" trumpet, rather it is a day of blowing many trumpets and of *shouting*. Both are images of a call for help:

> When you go into battle in your own land against an enemy who is oppressing you, sound a blast on the trumpets. Then you will be remembered by Eyahuwah Elahim and rescued from your enemies. Numbers 10:9

This day holds very significant prophetic importance for the end of our age, as we shall see.

The Day of Atonement always falls on the 10th day of the seventh month and this would be on sixth day of the week. It is a High Day and a day of fasting. On this day the one responsible for all the deception and trouble on earth will be set apart and the sins placed on his head. He will be taken away to a place where no person lives. This is the fallen messenger Azazel and who is represented by a goat. This is described in detail in Leviticus 16.

The Azazel goat, also called the scapegoat, is not, as many in the Christian religions like to believe, an image of Jesus' sacrifice. Azazel was the chief among the "angels that sinned" and led the people of the earth into such trouble that it had to be brought to an end at the close of the second age.

Although the sacrifices of the Day of Atonement are described in Leviticus, the understanding comes from the book of Enoch:

> And again the Lord said to Raphael: "Bind Azazel hand and foot, and cast him into the darkness: and make an opening in the desert, which is in Dudael, and cast him therein. And place upon him rough and jagged rocks, and cover him with darkness, and let him abide there forever, and cover his face that he may not see the light. And on the day of the great judgment he shall be cast into the fire. And heal the earth which the angels have corrupted, and proclaim the healing

of the earth, that they may heal the plague, and that all the children of men may not perish through all the secret things which the Watchers have disclosed and have taught their sons.

And the whole earth has been corrupted through the works that were taught by Azazel: to him ascribe all sin. 1 Enoch 10:4-8

By design the Bible raises more questions than answers, either because the knowledge behind the statements was already known, or because religious leaders suppressed knowledge, or because it is a good thing for the wise to seek out knowledge and truth. The passage above contains essential knowledge regarding the Day of Atonement. Without it people make mistakes when they try to understand the importance of the Day of Atonement.

The Feast of Tabernacles or Booths always begins on the 15th day, which occurs on the middle day of the week. It is a High day and the Feast continues for seven days. During this time the people live in temporary homes. It is an image of our transitory life on earth in the flesh while we await our permanent home. It also is an image of the 1,000 year (millennium) reign after the return of Eyahuwah/Eyahushuah. In the next age, the eighth, all the people of the earth must celebrate the Feast of Tabernacles. Those who refuse will suffer drought and plagues. (Zech. 14).

The Last Great Day of the Feast always falls on the 22nd day. It is a High day. It is also on the fourth day of the week. It is a separate feast from the Feast of Tabernacles. This is a time of great rejoicing as it is an image of salvation for the world and the time when death is no more.

These are the Feasts and High Days as set apart in the Torah. Moses knew what was written by his father, Enoch, including the structure of the Revealed Calendar, and how the Feasts and High Days were aligned with it. Since then the offspring of Israel substituted strange and foreign calendars upon which they placed whatever feasts, sabbaths, and high days appealed to them. The post exilic prophets spoke to the people, who, after returning, considered the Law to be too burdensome for them and created substitute laws of their own imaginations. This is true not only of the House of Judah, but also the Christian House of Israel, wherever they are in the world.

Seventh Month

			1 TR	2	3	4
5	6	7	8	9	10 AT	11
12	13	14	15 FT	16	17	18
19	20	21	22 GD	23	24	25
26	27	28	29	30		

Eighth Month

					1	2
3	4	5	6	7	8	9
10	11	12	13	14	15	16
17	18	29	20	21	22	23
24	25	26	27	28	29	30

Ninth Month

1	2	3	4	5	6	7
8	9	10	11	12	13	14
15	16	17	18	19	20	21
22	23	24	25	26	27	28
29	30	31				

KEY TO THE THIRD QUARTER OF THE CALENDAR
  TR: Fall Equinox, Feast of Trumpets; High Day
  AT: Day of Atonement, Day of Fasting; High Day
  FT: Start of Feast of Tabernacles; High Day; Seven Days
  GD: Last Great Day; High Day

The Problem of Keeping the Sabbath and the Feasts

According to Genesis, the Creator, on the fourth day of the week, set the sun, moon and stars for determining seasons and times. This then became the day when the recording of time on earth and the calendar started. The Creator created the Sabbath at the beginning. The fourth day of the week started the clock and the calendar. The Sabbath, the seventh day, started at sunset three days later.

Because there are more days in a year now, there is a problem trying to keep the Sabbath day. We now have too many days in the year to make the weeks come out nicely at 52 exact weeks in a year. Because the revealed calendar also determined the weekly Sabbath Days, there is a great conflict between the seventh day of the week on our calendars and the weekly Sabbath on the Revealed Calendar. The Sabbath, established before the flood, fell on the same day numbers in each year. The Sabbath always came on the 4th, 11th, 18th, 25th, etc., days of the year. And the Sabbath was always the Seventh day of the week.

Look at the revealed calendar and you can see how the Sabbath will stay aligned year after year forever, as long as you consider 364 days in the year. This is simply because the year consists of 52 full weeks. The actual elapsed time between the spring equinoxes remained the same now as before the flood. The only problem, as we have seen, is that the earth spins faster now! As a result, we now have a junk day in our solar year. To make the Feasts, Holy Days, and weekly Sabbath stay on the "clean" days, we must skip the extra day and treat it as an annual intercalary (not counted) day and not include that day as a weekday. There is no direct Law that declares what we do with this extra day. We are stuck with it. It is a "non-day" and a cursed day.

The Law of the calendar requires that the year start on the same day of the week forever until the creation of the new heaven and the new earth and that the year is exactly 52 weeks long. The new year always starts on the spring equinox. To find when to keep the Feasts and Holy Days we count days from the first day of the first and seventh months. The Passover is on the 14th day. The Days of Unleavened Bread start on the 15th day, and end on the 21st day. In the seventh month, the first day is the Feast of Trumpets. Atonement is the 10th day. Feast of Booths starts on the 15th day. The Last Great Day is the 22nd.

To find the Feast of Firstfruits and Weeks we count seven full weeks after the weekly Sabbath that comes *after* the day of the Wave Sheaf offering. The chief priest always offers the Wave Sheaf on the first day of the week during the Feast of Unleavened Bread. The Feast of Weeks always falls on the first day of the week. And this Feast is always 75 days or two and one-half months into the year. A full week starts on the first day of the week and ends at the end of the Sabbath. This is the Law of the calendar and no design of our own creation can change it. It is based on the sun and not the moon.

We must make an adjustment in our understanding. Regardless of how many times the earth spins on its axis during the year, we must understand that, in the Spirit, there are really only 364 days in the true year. We simply do not experience those days, but something close to them. The confusion is the result of human wickedness. It is another of the consequences of the great flood – "the first end."

The Law of the Feasts and High Days makes these days relative to the spring and fall equinoxes. This makes it possible to keep both these days and the weekly Sabbath on "clean" days.

All of these Feasts and Sacred Solemn Assemblies, Sabbaths and Holy days were set apart as "lasting ordinances for the generations to come, wherever you live!" Some attempt to keep them on "unclean" and profane days, rather than on the days appointed. They make up calendars that are convenient for them. Eyahuwah calls these, "Your feasts, your Sabbaths."

Scriptures confirm that the Feasts and Holy Days should be kept "throughout the generations, wherever you live." Prophecy says that they will be kept in the future, and very likely, in the near future, in our lifetime. Prophecy also shows that these days are not only for the descendants of Abraham, but also for all people in every nation. [See Zechariah 14]

To try to keep these days on any day that is convenient for us is a violation against us, according to both the Law and the Prophets. According to the following Scriptures, to claim to observe the Sabbath on a day that is not the Sabbath is an act of profanity. These also state that the priests really do not pay attention to what is clean and unclean:

> "You have despised My Holy things [including Holy Days] and profaned My Sabbaths." Ezekiel 22:8.
>
> "Son of man, say to her [My People], You are an unclean land ... " Ezekiel 22:24.
>
> "Her priests have violated My Teaching: They have profaned what is sacred [Holy] to Me. They have not distinguished between the sacred and the profane. They have not taught the difference between the unclean and the clean, and they have closed their eyes to *My* Sabbaths. I am profaned in her midst. Her officials are like wolves rending prey in her midst; they shed blood and destroy lives to win ill-gotten

gain. Her prophets, too, daub the wall for them with plaster. They prophesy falsely and divine deceitfully for them. They say, 'Thus says the Lord God, when the Lord [Eyahuwah] has not spoken. " Ezekiel 22:26-28 JSB.

"When you come to meet with Me, who has asked this of you, this trampling of my courts? Stop bringing meaningless offerings! Your incense is detestable to me. *Your new moons, sabbaths* and *convocations* – I cannot bear *your* evil assemblies. *Your* new moon festivals and *your* appointed feasts my soul hates. They have become a burden to me; I am weary of bearing them. *When you spread out your hands in prayer, I will hide my eyes from you; even if you offer many prayers, I will not listen."* Isaiah 1.

But now the Jews' feast of the tabernacles was near. His [Jesus's] brothers said to him, "Leave here and go up to Judea, that your disciples may also see your works. ... If you do these things, manifest yourself to the world." For neither did his brothers believe in him. So Jesus said to them, "My time is not yet come, but your time is always ready. The world is not able to hate you, but me it hates, because I bear witness concerning it that the works of it are evil. You go up to this feast. I am not going up to *this* feast, for my time is not yet fully come." And having said these things to them, he remained in Galilee.

But when his brothers were gone up, then he also went up to the Feast. John 7:2-10.

This is a literal translation from the Greek, because the Greek makes a distinction between the feast of the Jews, which Jesus called "*this* feast" and "*the Feast* of Tabernacles." The feast of the Jews, according to Pharisee traditions and teachings, and the Feast according to the Revealed Calendar were out of sync and were not the same feasts!

The Jews started their months with the new moon. The full moon of their seventh month was particularly important to them as it also meant the start of their new year. Josephus wrote that the Jews set up signal fires on the hills surrounding Jerusalem and watchers to spot the first sliver of the new moon. When a watcher saw the new moon he lit the signal fire. It took more than one day to determine the new moon. The only problem with this method was that the Romans also set fake signal fires to poke fun at the Jews.

But the seventh month of the Revealed Calendar starts with the fall equinox without regard for the phases of the moon. We find the same care given to the day of Pentecost (Feast of Weeks and Firstfruits) after Jesus' resurrection:

And when the day of Pentecost was *fully* come... Acts 2.1.

The only way to keep the Feasts and Holy or High Days and the weekly Sabbath day is to restart the new year on the spring Equinox making that day the fourth day of the week and the first day of the year and the first day of the first month. Then we may need to reset the year again at the time of the fall equinox making that day the first day of the seventh month and the fourth day of the week and the first day of the seventh month. This makes our extra day and a quarter a "non-day."

Although our day is shorter by five minutes from the length of the day in Enoch's age this doesn't matter when you consider that sunsets rather than hours and minutes measure the day. But it is necessary to align each new year and each half-year to keep in sync with the equinoxes because we now have "unclean" 1.242 days in our year. This extra time is twice unclean and observing it as a "day" on the Revealed Calendar only leads to confusion and corruption. Today, we can only follow the Revealed Calendar by synchronizing with the spring and fall equinoxes. During the time of Jesus and the apostles, the Essenes at Qumran tracked both calendars: the calendar of the Jews and the calendar revealed to Enoch.

We have a revealed list of ages or "weeks" that prophesy about specific events through the entire time of human history. We saw how the Feasts and High Days fit on the Revealed Calendar. Each of the special days is an image of prophetic importance to the entire world. Placing the Feasts and the weekly Sabbath on the Revealed calendar makes all those days clean.

The material in this chapter gives us enough information to find the start and end of the 1,335 days. We must learn how to count the 1,335 days because it is important to know where they start and end. Then we will know why there is a blessing associated with waiting for the end of the 1,335 days. As we shall see, what happens at the end of the 1,335 days is so shocking it will forever change the course of human history. If the coming of the Holy Spirit on Pentecost was revolutionary, wait until you see what is prophesied to happen at the end of the 1,335 days!

II

From Here to Kingdom Come!

Understand the Prophecies

And I heard, but I did not understand, so I said, "My Master, what is the latter end of these matters?"

And he said, "Go, Daniel, for the words are hidden and sealed till the time of the end. Many shall be cleansed and made white, and refined. But the wrong shall do wrong, and none of the wrong shall understand. But those who have insight shall understand." Daniel 12:8-10

Enoch, called "the Scribe of Righteousness" is the Father of all who dwell on the earth. We are all his offspring!

7 An End For Our Age

Many prophecy buffs and TV preachers tried to set dates for supernatural events only to show themselves mistaken as their dates passed without incident. Some preachers "prophesied" that Jesus was going to "rapture" the "church" away in some year, like 2000 or 2007, at the time of the Jewish Feast of Trumpets. Those date came and passed without incident. So the followers had to come down off of their hill, go home and wait for the next date. Not only were the preachers wrong about that date, but also about many other things as well. Hopefully, many learned a good lesson.

It is more important to know and understand the signs of the times, rather than trying to guess at dates on a civil calendar. Many people became fanatic about the year 2000, which turned out to be more noise, even to computer experts trying to deal with the century change from 19xx to 20xx. Either that or, like a military inspection to help justify chores to the troops, they found a good excuse to update computer software and equipment.

Prophesied times and events are based only upon the revealed calendar given to Enoch. The only way we can know where we are is to sync up our lives with the revealed calendar at the spring and fall equinoxes. Forget about trying to link up Scriptural prophecies with our current calendars. It can't be done. These calendars mean nothing

There are, however, other indicators that have come down through the centuries to give us some idea as to times that some believed to be important.

Here are some of those.

Physical Calendars

The Aztec and Mayan calendar produced a date that they believed would be a time of dramatic change on the earth. This was based upon certain periodic episodes in the history of the earth. One of these was calculated to happen in our lifetime. That date corresponds to the December 21 or 23, 2012 (winter solstice) on our calendar. To the Mayans and Aztecs, this was a time when their calendar completed a grand cycle that started, they believed, from creation. They believed this to be a time of great cataclysmic change on earth.

The Aztecs and Mayas studied the stars and constellations and our galaxy, which is also called the Milky Way. They discovered that our solar system travels in an orbit around the core the galaxy. This orbit crosses the equator of the galaxy – a focal point of energy emanating out from the galaxy's core. As we approach the galactic equator the earth may begin to experience events in the weather, electromagnetic transmissions, and possible solar events as a result of increases in cosmic dust entering the solar system.

In the year 2012, at the time of the winter solstice, the sun and the earth will be in the plane of the equator of our galaxy. There is a vast section of our galaxy known as the Dark Rift. The cause of the darkness is an enormous cloud of cosmic dust. No light passes through this section. So for our optical telescopes this section contains no stars. If the cosmic dust is thick we could experience a blackening of the heavens. The moon would appear as the color of blood, the sun darkened, and the stars not visible in a clear sky. In their place would be a constant display of meteoric showers as dust and larger particles burn up in the atmosphere.

As noted, great clouds of cosmic dust particles drawn into the sun by gravity become fuel causing the sun to give out extremely large solar flares and increased heat. This can cause the oceans to boil and great clouds of water vapor ascend into the stratosphere and the earth's rotation speed to slow down. These events may not happen exactly on that date, but that may only signify the beginning of the change. Because this is an event never before experienced by Man, we can only speculate about what would happen as the earth travels through the equator of the Milky Way. But the prophecies say:

> Immediately after the distress of those days, the sun will be darkened, and the moon will not give its light; the stars of heaven will fall from the sky, and the heavenly bodies will be shaken. At that time the sign of the Son of Man will appear in the sky, and all the nations of the earth will mourn. They will see the Son of Man coming on the clouds of the sky, with power and great glory. And he will send his angels [messengers] with a loud trumpet call, and they will gather his elect

from the four winds from one end of heaven to another. Matthew 24.29-31 NIV

See, the day of the Lord is coming – a cruel day, with wrath and fierce anger – to make the land desolate and destroy the sinners within it. The stars of heaven and their constellations will not show their light. The rising sun will be darkened and the moon will not give its light. ... Therefore *I will make the heavens tremble* and the earth will shake from its place at the wrath of Eyahuwah Almighty in the day of his burning anger. Isaiah 13:9-10,13 NIV

"Signs in the Sun and Moon"

The Delta Phenomenon – The Hidden Order in All Markets by Welles Wilder is a study of the activity of financial markets and their relation to natural phenomenon. According to the study, there appears to be a strong correlation between the relationship between the sun, moon and earth and both the commodities and stock markets. The Delta Phenomenon was uncovered by research performed by Jim Sloman. Essentially, it shows that stock and commodity markets are related to both macro and micro relationships between the sun, moon, and earth, and human emotions. Because the markets are very often influenced by human emotions and because human emotions are influenced by astronomical events, it appears possible that markets can be predicted once we can determine the patterns and find their relationship to the various financial markets.

For example, one relationship between the markets and the sun, moon and earth is "Markets repeat directly or inversely relative to the total interaction of the sun, moon and earth". More specifically, "Markets repeat directly or inversely every four lunar months." One of the Deltas is called the Super Long Term Delta (SLTD), which is, "every complete total interaction of the sun, moon and earth — every 19 years and 5 hours." This corresponds to the Jewish lunar calendar, which is repeated every 19 years.

If markets are affected by the sun, moon, and earth, so is everything else in human life. The markets help provide some veracity to the Delta Phenomenon because of the vast amount of detailed history accumulated by trading and the large number of people engaged in that activity. But like the financial markets other recurring events also provide sufficient history to provide patterns.

Wars and Battles Between Nations

By creating a collection of dates for wars for the past 300 years, it is possible to overlay the SLTD and uncover a correlation. And having done that, extend it to the future to pinpoint times when major wars might happen. To my surprise, a repeated pattern began to emerge quickly. -Extending this into the future, a time appeared as a possible time for a major world war. That time was the year 2012 – the same year important to the Aztecs.

Signs in the Planets

The book *Rosslyn — Guardian of the Secrets of the Holy Grail* by Tim Wallace-Murphy and Marilyn Hopkins proposed another special event. The book is an account of research surrounding the Rosslyn Chapel in Scotland – a very unusual "unfinished" cathedral that is believed by some to include important historical treasures and documents and spiritual power.

The authors include an account of a pilgrimage they took visiting historical spiritual sites in Europe. These sites dated back to the Druids and have remained important locations for some people since that time. Cathedrals were built upon these locations. Each location was also historically associated with these heavenly bodies: The Moon, Mercury, Venus, The Sun, Mars, Jupiter, and Saturn. The corresponding locations are: Cathedral of St. James at Compostela in Spain, Notre-Dame de Dalbade in Toulouse France, Orleans Cathedral in France, Chartres Cathedral in France, Notre-Dame de Paris, Amiens Cathedral in France, and Rosslyn Chapel in Scotland. The account of the spiritual experiences of the authors at these locations is interesting. But what I found fascinating was their conclusion regarding the significance of associating each location with the sun, moon and planets.

> Trevor had been convinced that when the relationship of the planets in the heavens represented that of the seven planetary oracles in our configuration, this would herald a time of cataclysmic change. We had to ascertain whether this replication was even possible. If it were to prove viable, then, perhaps, the chapel would disclose another secret – the date of apocalyptic change. Surprisingly, we did find a date on which not only did the planets align themselves in the order of the sites, but when we compared the print-out to one of

our large-scale maps covering a major portion of the northern hemisphere, the replication was almost exact. The date of this alignment in the heavens is one that falls well within the lifetime of most of our readers.

The question was "Is there a time in the future, when these bodies at the same time will be aligned with the earth in such a way that a vertical or zenith projection from each sight will point to the corresponding body represented by that location?" They found, after some research and calculations, a date when that would happen. According to their calculations, that event would occur on July 28, 2019.

Whether or not there is any merit to their research can only be judged in retrospect or at least by others who perform the same research. I cannot confirm that what they found is true, but it is interesting.

Target Earth!

On March 8, 2002, asteroid 2002 EM7 passed within 288,000 miles of Earth. Because it came from a "blind spot" near the sun, it was not seen until it passed by! Recently, one passed by that was closer. In June 14, 2002, asteroid 2002 MN passed within 74,000 miles of the earth – and it also wasn't seen until it had passed us! But according to astronomers, Asteroid 2002 NT7 is on a path that will lead it to a possible collision with the earth in the year 2019! I do not have the resources to confirm any significance to planet alignment in July of 2019. And I invite any who can either confirm or deny an event like this to pass the information along to the publishers.

The 1335 days of Daniel was something that was "hidden" and "concealed" until the time of the end. Even Daniel didn't understand the information given to him.

> Jesus said, *"There will be signs in the sun, moon, and stars (planets). On the earth, nations will be in anguish and perplexity at the roaring and tossing of the sea. Men will faint from terror, apprehensive of what is coming on the world, for the heavenly bodies will be shaken. At that time they will see the Son of Man coming in a cloud with power and great glory. When these things begin to take place, stand up and lift up your heads, because your redemption is drawing near."*

We have examined some dates that came to us from current research and from history. It seems significant that there is a seven-year time period between 2012 and 2019. Later as those days draw nearer or afterward, we will see that these dates did or did not relate to important events prophesied long ago.

Considering what is happening now in the world, we can do this: You and I can prepare for the changes that were prophesied. But this time the preparation may have little to do with earthquake kits, food and water storage, and weapons caches. The real preparation is spiritual. It starts within you and me.

The Prophetic Revealed Calendar

From here on I will also call Enoch's revealed calendar the Prophetic Calendar, because it contains within it days and feasts that prophesy the future of the human race. We examined the Prophetic Calendar as revealed to Enoch and found that it was declared to be in force "for all the years of the world unto eternity, till the new creation is accomplished which endures all eternity." We found that the Feasts and Holy Days described in the Law fit with precision and structure within the Prophetic Calendar. Given all these details and facts we must conclude that the 1,335 days relates directly to the Prophetic Calendar and its Special Sacred Days in their "clean" and proper place.

Then we saw that Enoch also had a vision that covered the history of the human race for all eternity. Out of the many "weeks" in this vision, seven were devoted to what would happen to the world until the "change" comes.

We also took a good look at some important happenings during the age in which we now live and must conclude that we are living in the end of the seventh age. So we should expect to gain insight into things that were hidden for this day and time.

Waiting time is over ...

We are now ready to uncover the seal and understand the real meaning of the prophecies of Daniel.

THE WOMAN CLOTHED WITH THE SUN

A great and wondrous sign appeared in heaven: a woman clothed with the sun, with the moon under her feet and a crown of twelve stars on her head. Revelation 12:1

The woman represents the nation of Israel as a united group made up of all the descendents of the sons of Jacob: Judah, Reuben, Gad, Asher, Naphtali, Joseph [represented by his sons Ephraim and Manasseh], Simeon, Levi, Issachar, Zebulun, Benjamin, and Dan. These twelve are symbolized by the crown of twelve stars on her head. The nation of Israel was split into two nations, the House of Israel and the House of Judah, during the reign of Solomon's son. But spiritually there never was any division to Elahim and Eyahuwah as the Nations of Israel will be united again in the eighth age.

The sun as clothing and the 12-star crown shows the important place of the 12-month solar calendar with the Feasts and Holy Days revealed to Enoch and Moses. The moon *under her feet* represents the subordinate position the moon holds to the Nations of Israel

8 Revisiting Daniel's Visions

The end of the our age, the Seventh week of Enoch's vision, has now been made clear through the revelations *given to* Daniel and John the Apostle. For the first time these end time prophecies are unsealed. The key to unlocking the mystery of the ages lies in understanding the revelations that were at first given to our father Enoch, and then later to Daniel, and finally to the Apostle John. However, all of these things had been sealed up until the time of the "second end" – our time.

In this chapter and in the next few I will show the map of the events that bring us to the end of our age and the start of the Eighth age. This is a fascinating study, particularly because this subject has been a target of mindless speculations and traditions.

ENOCH'S CALENDAR: THE KEY TO PROPHECY

Some chafe at the idea that Enoch, the father of us all, could have any importance during our time. The desire for religious dominance over the mind of the masses has stupefied the people into thinking that Enoch was "done away" because he was not part of the "Canon." But Enoch prophesied that his words would be a part of understanding at this time in history. The key to prophecy is the 364-day calendar revealed to Enoch by the Messenger from Elahim, Gabriel. This calender always starts on the fourth day of the week and on the spring equinox, the day when the length of the day is the same as the length of the night. The calendar has four quarters of ninety-one days, which is the same as thirteen weeks. Thus all quarters start on the fourth day of the week. To make this work out nicely, the last month in each quarter has thirty-one days. The first and second months of the quarters have thirty days each. Only 360 days of each year are to be counted. The last day of each quarter is not included in the counting as we shall see.

I explained how the earth's year length was changed to 365.242 days, not by getting struck by a comet and slowing down the orbital speed (Velikovsky's idea). But rather a change in the atmosphere caused the earth's rotation speed to increase by a small amount. Up until the 1930s scientists assumed that the earth's rotation speed was an unchangeable constant, but that proved to be false. Today NASA and other scientists keep track of the changes of rotation speed and found that weather can either speed up or slow down the rotation. This continual observation is needed for calculating trajectories required for space exploration.

As noted, the change happened as a result of the great flood when the "waters above" the troposphere came back down to the earth, and like an ice skater pulling her arms in while doing a pirouette, the earth rotated faster. We now have another intercalary day of 1.242 days at the end of Enoch's year, but each year still starts on the spring equinox whether we believe or not.

Daniel's Messages from Gabriel

Like Enoch, Daniel also had contact with Gabriel. Daniel was given periods of time expressed as days. What most "wannabe prophets" miss, because they don't have a clue about Enoch and his writings, is that the same Gabriel who revealed the calendar also revealed the time periods to Daniel. Daniel was given these messages:

The first message sets the context and then jumps to the time of trouble at the end of our age. From Daniel 8, The Scriptures:

> Out of one of them came another horn [kingdom], which started small but grew in power to the south and to the east and toward the Beautiful Land [Israel]. It grew until it reached the host of the heavens, and it threw some of the starry host down to the earth and trampled on them. It set itself up to be as great as the Prince of the host. It took away the daily sacrifice from him, and the place of his sanctuary was brought low. Because of the rebellion, the host [armies] of the chosen and the daily sacrifice were given over to it. It prospered in everything it did, and truth was thrown to the ground.
>
> Then I heard a holy one speaking, and another holy one said to him, "How long will it take for the vision to be fulfilled – the vision concerning the daily sacrifice, the rebellion that

causes desolation, and the surrender of the sanctuary and of the host that will be trampled underfoot?"

He said to me, "It will take 2,300 evenings and mornings, then the sanctuary will be reconsecrated."

Evening and morning is the same as one day as we learn from Genesis 1 where the very same expression in the Hebrew is used. Now for those who want to convert these to years: hold off. No where was Daniel told to count "a day for a year." Ezekiel was told to do this because he was instructed to act out something and each day of his duty was to count for one year of actual time. It was this "day for year" misapplication of the 2,300 evenings and mornings that led some to think that "a rapture" was to happen on June 12, 2007 or some other imagined date. Sometimes people go to great lengths to deceive themselves.

As we shall see, the expression "evening and morning" is an actual day in time on Enoch's calendar. The difference is that *this period of time includes the intercalary days which are not counted otherwise*. The daily sacrifice was to be carried out for each day regardless of its place on the calendar. These then are actual days as counted by sunsets and sunrises as opposed to calendar days that only count 360 days per year.

While I, Daniel, was watching the vision and trying to understand it, there before me stood one who looked like a man. And I heard a man's voice from the Ulai [river] calling, "Gabriel, tell this man the meaning of the vision."

As he came near the place where I was standing, I was terrified and fell prostrate. "Son of man," he said to me, "understand that *the vision concerns the time of the end."*

As noted, many mistakes in understanding resulted from trying to "understand" this vision by converting the 2,300 evenings and mornings to years. We are not going to make that mistake, because this vision concerns our time and the end of our age.

He [Gabriel] said, "*I am going to tell you what will happen later in the time of wrath because the vision concerns the appointed time of the end."*

"The two-horned ram that you saw represents the kings of Media and Persia [Iran]. The shaggy goat is the king of Greece, and the large horn between his eyes is the first king [Alexander]. The four horns that replaced the one that was broken off represent four kingdoms that will emerge from his nation but will not have the same power."

This sets the context but not the time. The four kingdoms are the Seleucid empires that took over that region after Alexander. The presence of the four kingdoms has remained. And the vision now jumps to our time:

> "*In the latter part of their reign,* when rebels have become completely wicked, a stern faced king, a master of intrigue, will arise. He will become very strong, but not by his own power. He will cause astounding devastation and will succeed in whatever he does. He will destroy the mighty men [armies] and the holy [chosen] people. He will cause deceit to prosper, and he will consider himself superior. When they [the rebels] feel secure, he will destroy many and take his stand against the Prince of princes. Yet he will be destroyed but not by human power.
>
> "The vision of the evenings and mornings that has been given to you is true, *but seal up the vision for it concerns the distant future.*" Daniel 8 NIV

That "distant future" is now. It is amazing to see how the key statements about the time spoken of in the prophecy are ignored! This is the first time period that will become part of the end-time schedule. The others follow.

Daniel 9: The End of the Sixth Age

Enoch wrote about the Sixth Age:

> And after that in the Sixth Week all who live in it shall be blinded. And the hearts of all of them shall godlessly forsake wisdom. And in it a man shall ascend. And at its close the house of dominion shall be burnt with fire, and the whole race of the chosen root shall be dispersed.

Daniel's Ninth Chapter and the 70 Weeks

As noted, the ninth chapter of Daniel concerns another time of the end: the end of the sixth age. This ninth chapter has been mistakenly used to point to the coming of Jesus. However, once again, the truth has been set aside for tradition and fables. Daniel was never told that the seventy weeks were to be expanded to 490 years. Instead, the Hebrew says that the weeks were to be *divided up, intersected, or parsed* to fit events. It serves as an example of how Daniel's other visions were to be used.

Briefly, Agrippa was the one who made an "agreement or covenant with the mighty", the Romans. They then laid siege against Jerusalem and a war started that was to last for seven years. In the midst of that seven years, the sacrifices ceased and the temple was burned to the ground. After the seven-years war ended, for sixty-two years the Romans occupied Jerusalem. They made it into an army camp complete with "ditches" or latrines. It was also a time of continual trouble in Jerusalem and in the l and.

Near the end of the sixty-two weeks, a "messiah" came on the scene and began a rebellion of the Jews against the Romans. Rabbi Akiba called the man, Simon Bar Kokhba, the "Son of the Star" and declared him to be the promised messiah. For three and one-half years they fought against the Romans making the Roman occupation miserable. But the Romans prevailed and defeated the rebels and the Jews suffered huge losses. Bar Kokhba was cut off in the "middle of a week" of years and found hiding in a cave in En-Gedi with no one to help him. At the end of 69 of the 70 weeks, it was over. The people of the Jews were dispersed and forbidden to enter Jerusalem and were "encouraged" to flee the country. The sixth age ended as Enoch and Daniel saw in their visions and recorded for our day.

Daniel 12: More End of the Age Prophecies

Along with Zechariah 14, Daniel 12 is one of the most direct prophesies about the end of the age, our age. The information in this chapter needs to be combined with the information of the eighth chapter and with some material from John's visions. With that we can create the time line of end time events.

There is some confusion about the remaining week of Daniel 12. Some call what I am about to write, the "lost week theory." Those who object to this are usually the same who defend the "day for a year" notion of Daniel 9 to try to make it point to Jesus. But Daniel's vision of the weeks is clear in stating that the "70 weeks" must be intersected or divided up as the Hebrew word explains. No expansion is even suggested. Instead it is only assumed. In fact, there is little hard evidence even from the New Testament as to how long Jesus' ministry was. Was it one year - from Passover to Passover - as John seems to suggest? Or could it have been three and one half years as some say Daniel 9 means? But then that cannot be substantiated either, and when we apply that "theory" we have the tail wagging the dog.

For our purposes here, we can use the one week that was "cut out" or "divided" from the other weeks and apply it to our time. After all, **the weeks of Daniel 9 were to be applied to his people**, and not to an individual. The gospel writer said concerning Daniel, "Let the reader understand."

And so we will.

9 Forward to the End

After examining Enoch's calendar and some of the message given to Daniel by Gabriel, we must continue to show how Daniel's and John's visions come together at the end of our age. Surprisingly, there are some who think that all of these prophecies have been fulfilled at some time in the past. Those who are convinced of these fables are in for a big surprise. Some, influenced by Paul the Pharisee and his private interpretations, reject "Old Testament" scriptures as unnecessary documents. Others think that Jesus has already returned. We must remember that the gospel is a product of understanding the Scriptures including the Torah, the Prophets and the Writings from which the Apostles preached their message. They were not followers of Paul and they did not teach anything using Paul's writings as a source. But they did quote from the writings of Enoch, which raised these to level of Scripture.

DANIEL 10: THE TARGET OF THE REVELATIONS

The prophecies of Daniel 10 and 11 expand on the events yet to occur in our time.

> And he [Gabriel] said to me, "O Daniel, man greatly appreciated, understand the words that I speak to you, and stand upright, for I have now been sent to you," And while he was speaking this word to me, I stood trembling.
>
> And he said to me, "Do not fear, Daniel, for from the first day that you set your heart to understand and to humble yourself before your Elahim, your words were heard, and I have come because of your words.
>
> "But the head of the rule of Persia [Iran] withstood me twenty-one days. And see, Michael, one of the chief heads, came to help me, for I had been left alone there with the sov-

ereigns of Persia.

"And I have come to make you understand what is to befall your people in the latter days. For the vision is yet for days to come."

And he said, "Do you know why I have come to you? And now I return to fight with the head of Persia. And when I have left, see, the head of Greece shall come.

"But let me declare to you what is written in the Scripture of Truth, and there is no one supporting me against these, except Michael, your head."

Chapter 11 of Daniel continues this message about what will take place to Daniel's people in the latter days, which as we shall see is our time. There were events that happened in Daniel's day and afterward, but the core of this vision is for the latter days. Daniel lived during the sixth age revealed to Enoch. The message given to Daniel covered events that happened during that age. These events laid the foundation for what is about to happen at the end of the seventh age, and immediately prior to the beginning of the eighth age. Don't be fooled by any who claim that righteousness rules today. Wickedness in this world is increasing at geometric rates and is about to consume the nations.

Daniel 11: Crossing troubled waters

Because chapter 11 contains so much information I can only quote a portion of it here. But the messenger gave us instruction concerning the context. There are wars on earth and there are wars in heaven. The messengers Gabriel and Michael have joined forces to resist those who are stirring up evil in the world. The prophecies of Chapter 11 are written in that context and cover centuries leading to our time. These events include the domination of Rome [Kittim] during the sixth age.

Like Gabriel and Michael, there are other spiritual beings and leaders who influenced and help the rogue nations of the Middle East, and the results of their efforts are recorded in Chapter 11. Given that, we now move on to the prophecies that focus on our time now.

Gabriel continues:

"At the appointed time he shall return and go toward the south, but it shall not be like the former or the latter. For ships from Kittim [Roman Empire] shall come against him, and he shall lose heart, and shall return in rage against the set-apart covenant, and shall act, and shall return and consider those who forsake the set-apart covenant. And strong ones shall arise from him and profane the set-apart place, the stronghold, and shall take away that which is continual, and set up the abomination that lays waste. [The events of the 70 weeks prophecy]

"And by flatteries he shall profane those who do wrong against the covenant. But the people who know their Elahim shall be strong and shall act. And those of the people who have insight shall give understanding to many. And they shall stumble by sword and flame, by captivity and plundering for days.

"And when they stumble they shall be helped, a little help, but many shall join them by flatteries.

"And some of those who have insight shall stumble, to refine them, and to cleanse them, and to make them white, until the time of the end, for it is still for an appointed time."
Daniel 11:29-35 The Scriptures

This speaks of the time before, during, and after the end of the sixth age. During that time a great religious system was formed that appropriated the Name of the one we call Jesus and taught things that replaced the teachings of Eyahushuah [Jesus] and the Apostles, and the Torah, the Prophets and the Writings. The Age of Apostasy was created as Enoch saw in his vision:

And after that in the seventh week [age] shall an apostate generation arise, and many shall be its deeds, and all its deeds shall be apostate. Enoch 93:9

Now Gabriel, after laying the foundation and the context, moves to the events of our day.

"And the ruler [of Persia] shall do as he pleases and shall exalt himself and show himself to be great above every mighty one [Elah], and speak incredible matters against the EL of the mighty ones [Elahim], and shall prosper until the wrath has been accomplished – for what has been decreed shall be done – and have no regard for the mighty ones [Elahim] of his fathers nor for the desire of women, nor have any regard for any mighty one [Elah[, but exalt himself above them all.

"But in his place he shall give esteem to a God of fortresses, and to a God that his fathers did not know he shall give esteem with gold and silver, with precious stones and costly gifts. And he shall act against the strongest strongholds with a foreign [strange] God which he shall acknowledge. He will greatly honor those who acknowledge him and cause them to rule over many and divide the land for gain.

"At the time of the end, the sovereign of the South shall push at him, and the sovereign of the North rush against him like a whirlwind, with chariots [armored vehicles], horsemen [armies], and with many ships. And he shall enter the lands and shall overflow and pass over, and shall enter the Splendid Land [Israel] and many shall stumble, but these escape from his hand: Edom, and Moab, and the chief of the sons of Ammon. And he shall stretch out his hand against the lands, and the land of Mitsrayim [Egypt] shall not escape. And he shall rule over the treasures of gold and silver, and over all the riches of Mitsrayim, and Libyans and Kushites shall be at his steps.

"Then reports from the east and the north shall disturb him, and he shall go out with great wrath to destroy and put many under the ban, and he shall pitch the tents of his palace between the seas and the splendid set-apart mountain [Jerusalem].

"But he shall come to his end with none to help him." Daniel 11:36-45 The Scriptures

Chapter 12 of Daniel continues the prophecies of the end of the seventh age given by Gabriel to Daniel to record for our time. It is in this chapter that we will find periods expressed as years and days. And we will also find events of great importance to the world as what is to follow will forever change government, politics, religion, longevity and peace.

DANIEL 12: EVENTS CLOSE THE SEVENTH WEEK

The first event to happen, after all of this trouble and wrath upon the earth and the chosen, Gabriel tells Daniel is that Michael will stand up to protect Daniel's people. Gabriel continues:

> "Now at that time Michael shall stand up, the great Head [Prince] who is standing over the sons of your people. And there shall be a time of distress, such as there never was since there was a nation until that time. And at that time your people shall be delivered, everyone who is found written in the book." Daniel 12:1 The Scriptures

Gabriel explains that Michael, once again, will take up the fight. This event is explained in the Book of Revelation:

> And there was war in heaven, Michael and his messengers [armies] fought against the dragon, and the dragon and his messengers [armies] fought back. But he was not strong enough, and they lost their place in heaven. The great dragon was hurled down, that great serpent called the devil or Satan, who leads the whole world astray. He was hurled to the earth, and his armies with him.

This was written about earlier in the exposition of the eighth chapter of Daniel:

> Out of one of them came another horn [kingdom], which started small but grew in power to the south and to the east and toward the Beautiful Land [Israel]. It grew until it reached the host of the heavens, and it threw some of the starry host down to the earth and trampled on them. It set itself up to be as great as the Prince of the host.

The last chapter of Daniel, like the other prophecies in Daniel, use a technique amusingly dubbed "hyper-baton." This is a reference to an orchestra conductor who wields an over active baton making it difficult for the listener to get a sense of the music. This was also used in the 70 weeks prophecy.

This chapter of Daniel's vision along with the Book of Revelation includes a number of important end-time events. The vision is almost a listing of events without regard for the order. But hidden within this is information that can help us establish the order, which has been sealed up until our time. This is information that Daniel did not know and neither did the Apostle John.

Gabriel told Daniel:

> "But you, go your way till the end. And rest, and arise to your lot at the end of the days."

Now we start putting the pieces together to see what this puzzle says.

10   Like Pieces of a Puzzle

We can now begin to take the pieces of information given to Daniel, Enoch, and John and, like a puzzle, put these together. Daniel's message, which he received from Gabriel ["strong Man of El"], was given in pieces that were not in order. It was left up to the wise to put the pieces together. The key to this task is understanding that the pieces were given to "men of El" over the millennia, and that these were sealed until the end time, about which they wrote. Enoch's book starts with this shocking message:

> The words of the blessing of Enoch, wherewith he blessed the elect [chosen] and the righteous, *who will be living in the day of tribulation*, when all the wicked and godless are to be removed. And he took up this parable and said, "Enoch, a righteous man, whose eyes were opened by Elah, saw the vision of the Holy [set apart] One in the heavens, which angels [messengers] showed me, and *from them I heard everything, and from them I understood as I saw, but not for this generation, but for a remote one which is for to come.*"

His message, like the messages given to Daniel and to John, are for us who are living at this time, the end of the seventh age.

> Concerning the elect [chosen] I said and took up my parable concerning them:
>
> The Holy Great One will come forth from His dwelling, and the eternal Elah will tread upon the earth, even on Mount Sinai, and appear from His camp, and appear in the strength of His might from the heaven of heavens, and all shall be smitten with fear! And the Watchers shall quake and great fear and trembling shall seize them unto the ends of the earth.
>
> And the high mountains [great nations] shall be shaken,

and the high hills [small nations] shall be made low and shall
melt like wax before the flame. The earth shall be wholly rent
in sunder, and all that is upon the earth shall perish and there
shall be a judgment upon all men.

Enoch continues to tell about the good things that will happen to the righteous and to the chosen [elect]:

But with the righteous He will make peace, and will protect the elect, and mercy shall be upon them. And they shall
all belong to Elah, and they shall be prospered, and they shall
all be blessed. And he will help them all, and light shall appear to them, and He will make peace with them.

What follows is a famous passage that was quoted in Jude 14 raising the writings of Enoch to the level of Scripture and Prophecy:

And behold! He comes with ten thousands of His holy
ones to execute judgment on all, and to destroy all the ungodly, and to convict all flesh of all their ungodliness which they
have ungodly committed, and of all the hard things which
ungodly sinners have spoken.

CLUES GIVEN TO DANIEL AND JOHN

Now from Daniel 12, Gabriel continues:

"Those who have insight shall shine like the brightness of
the expanse, and those who lead many to righteousness like
the stars forever and ever.

"But you, Daniel, hide the words, and seal the book *until
the time of the end*. Many shall diligently search and
knowledge shall increase."

Then, I, Daniel, looked and saw two others standing, one
on this bank of the river and the other on that bank. And one
said to the man dressed in linen, who was above the waters of
the river, "How long until the end of these wonders?"

And I heard the man dressed in linen, who was above the
waters of the river, and he held up his right hand and his left
hand to the heavens, and swore by Him who lives forever,
that *it would be for a time, times, and half a time. And when
they have ended scattering the power of the set-apart [chosen]*

people, then all these shall be completed.

There is a period of time [time, times and half a time] at the end of which ALL these thing shall be complete. A time is one year. Therefore, this is three and one half years or 1,260 days using the calendar revealed to Enoch. The phrase "All these things" means that all these events are included. The completion, however, comes at the end of three and one half years, after a great time of distress comes on Daniel's people (verse 1).

> And I heard but I did not understand, so I said, "My Master, what is the latter end of these matters?"
> And he said, "Go, Daniel, for *the words are hidden and sealed to the time of the end.* Many shall be cleansed and made white, and refined. But the wrong shall do wrong – and none of the wrong shall understand, *but those who have insight shall understand.*"

BELIEVE IT OR NOT, THESE WORDS ARE ABOUT TO BE UNSEALED.

Another clue or puzzle piece is given:

> "And from the time that which is continual is taken away, and the abomination that lays waste is set up, is 1,290 days."

There have been times in the past when an abomination was set up. One was set up by Antiochus Epiphanies, another after the dispersion of the people when Hadrian, who before gave the decree to "restore and rebuild Jerusalem," came and built Jerusalem and made it a place of worship to Capitoline Jupiter. But those were mere shadows of the coming abomination.

There is another piece that connects to this part of the puzzle: the 2,300 evening and mornings. This is referred to in Daniel 8 as related to "the continual," which is a reference to the evening and morning or daily sacrifices that were to be made forever. The phrase above "from the time that which is continual is taken away" connects the time to starting counting days to the time when the abomination that leads to desolation is set up. You count from the beginning of the 2,300 sequential days to 1,290 afterward on the Revealed Calender. Furthermore, the end of the 2,300 days will be the time of victory! It marks the end of our age!

So we now have *termini ad quem* pointing to the same day:
1. The END of the "time, times and half a time" (1,260 days).
2. The END of the 2,300 evenings and mornings.

And we have the time at the beginning of the 2,300 days when we can start counting days until the abomination that leads to desolation is set up: 1,290 days later.

Both the last three and one half years and the 2,300 evenings and mornings end at the same time. This is interesting, but there is not enough here to complete the puzzle. And we still have this:

> "Blessed is he who is waiting earnestly, and comes to the 1,335 days."

After this Daniel was told:

> "But you [Daniel], go your way till the end, and rest, and ARISE to your lot **at the end of the days.**"

The resurrection comes at the end of the days. The time of delivery comes at the end of the three and one half years, a time of great distress and trouble. From Daniel 12 alone we know that the people will be delivered and the resurrection will happen at the same time!

John's visions and the Secret of Elahim

From Revelation 10 starting at verse 5, we have a very familiar message, much like the message of Gabriel as noted above:

> And the messenger whom I saw standing on the sea and on the land lifted up his right hand to hand to the heaven and swore by Him who lives forever and ever, who created the heaven and what is in it, the earth and what is in it, and the sea and what is in it, that there shall be no further delay, **but in the days of the seventh messenger, when he is about to sound, the secret of Elahim shall also be ended, as He declared to His servants the prophets.**

We live in unusual times. The secret of Elahim has ended and you are about to learn what that is.

> And the voice which I heard out of the heaven spoke to me again and said, "Go, take the little book, which is opened in the hand of the messenger standing on the sea and on the earth. And I went to the messenger and said to him, "Give

me the little book." And he said to me, "Take and eat it, and it shall make your stomach bitter, but it shall be as sweet as honey in your mouth."

And I took the little book out the messenger's hand and ate it, and it was as sweet as honey in my mouth, but when I had eaten it, my stomach was made bitter. And he said to me, "You have to prophesy again concerning many peoples and nations and sovereigns [rulers]."

Then what follows are other keys that unlock this secret which started at first with Enoch, then with Daniel.

And a reed like a measuring rod was given to me, and the messenger stood, saying, "Rise and measure the Dwelling Place of Elahim [Temple or Tabernacle], and the altar and those worshipping in it. But *exclude the court which is outside the Dwelling Place [the Outer Court], and do not measure it,* for it has been given to the gentiles, and they shall trample the set-apart city [Jerusalem] under foot for *forty-two months*.

Forty-two months noted above is 3 times 12 months plus 6 more months or three and one-half years or 1,260 days. Months on Enoch's calendar contain 30 countable days.

Measuring of the Temple or Tabernacle was given both to John and Ezekiel in anticipation of a future time of construction. Now the mistake that I have seen is the assumption by some that these visions are of the same thing. But this not true. John was told to exclude and not measure the outer court area, whereas Ezekiel saw the Outer Court and its measurements:

... on that very day the hand of Eyahuwah was upon me and he took me there. In visions of Elah he took me to the land of Israel and set me on a very mountain, on whose south side were some buildings that looked like a city. He took me there, and I saw a man whose appearance was like bronze. He was standing in the gateway with a linen cord and a measuring rod in his hand.

Then *he brought me into the outer court.* There I saw some rooms and a pavement that had been constructed all around the court. There were thirty rooms along the pavement. It abutted the sides of the gateways and was as wide as they were long. This was the lower pavement. *Then he measured the distance from the inside of the lower gateway to the outside of the inner court.* It was a hundred cubits on the east side as well as on the north. Ezekiel 40.

Two witnesses prophesy for 1,260 days

The building of a Temple or Tabernacle can only happen before the time the daily sacrifices cease (2,300 evenings and mornings). Also concurrently or shortly after the worship starts, the two witnesses begin their time of prophecy that continues for 1,260 days or three and one half years. There is no time mentioned when a Temple or Tabernacle and Altar is constructed and worship starts. It could happen tomorrow. If I were to make a guess, I think it might happen after the Palestinian (Philistine) problem is mollified. The people of the Jews would then feel more at ease. We must wait and see what happens.

Who are the two witnesses?

"I shall give to my two witnesses, and they shall prophesy one thousand two hundred and sixty days clad in sackcloth."

These are the two olive trees and the two lamps that are standing before the ruler of the earth. And if anyone wishes to harm them, fire comes out of their mouth and consumes their enemies. And if anyone wishes to harm [kill] them, he has to be killed in the same way.

These possess authority to shut the heaven, so that no rain falls in the days of their prophecy. And they possess authority over the waters to turn them to blood, and to smite the earth with all plagues, as often as they wish.

However, the start of prophecy of the two witnesses is a major marker. Three and one half years (1,260 days) later, they are killed by the "beast".

And *when they have ended their witness,* the beast coming up out of the pit of the deep shall fight against them, and overcome them and kill them, and their dead bodies lie in the street of the great city which spiritually is called "Sodom and Mitsrayim [Egypt], where also their Master was impaled. For three and one half days people from every tribe, tongues, and nations will gaze on their dead bodies, and not allow their

> dead bodies to be placed into tombs. And those dwelling on the earth rejoice over them and exult. And they shall send gifts to each other, because these two prophets tormented those dwelling on the earth.

But their party will be cut short:

> And after the three and a half days, the spirit of life from the Elahim entered into them, and they stood upon their feet, and great fear fell on those who saw them. And they heard a loud voice from heaven saying to them, "Come up here." And they went up into heaven in a cloud, and their enemies saw them.

THE LAST THREE AND ONE HALF YEARS OF THE SEVENTH AGE

The two witnesses are also prophesied as the "Second Woe." After they finished their three and a half year witness and ascend to heaven, the third and final woe "comes speedily." The implication is that either the two witnesses finish at the end of the second woe, and the beast starts to make war with the chosen, elect and righteous immediately afterward. If so, then we have a seven year period defined. If there is a gap then we have one three and a half year period (two witnesses) separated from the last three and a half year period. The 70th week of Daniel 9 could be "divided" like this.

> The second woe has past, and see, the third woe comes speedily.

Chapter 12 of the Book of Revelation is a summary of the events found in Daniel 12. They also include the events of Zechariah 14, and Ezekiel 37 - 39.

The first verse describes a "sign in heaven." This is a very interesting verse because it relates to the end of this age using terms also used to explain the beginning of time.

> And Elahim said, "Let lights come to be in the expanse of the heavens to separate the days from the nights, and *let them be for signs and appointed times*, and for days and years, and let them be for lights in the expanse of the heavens to give light on the earth." And it came to be so. And Elahim made two great lights: the greater to rule the day, and the lesser to rule the night, and the stars. Genesis 1

Compare this with Revelation twelve:

> And a great sign was seen in the heaven: a woman clothed
> with the sun, with the moon under her feet, and on her head
> a crown of twelve stars.

Why the strong parallel between what is described in Genesis and in Revelation? The simplest answer is that the signs created at the very beginning were to be observed by the chosen and elect throughout eternity. We do not see that today because the people abandoned the teachings in exchange for a "different" idea taught by the sect or cult of the Pharisees. This sign is very clear, the people were, from the beginning, to be clothed with "the sun," the primary sign that would determine their future. That is the *solar* calendar revealed to Enoch and which was to contain the signs (the equinoxes, and solstices which marked the quarters), appointed times (Feasts and High Days), and days (Sabbaths) and years (the seventh years and the Jubilee years).

The moon is the "lesser light" and has a subordinate position under her feet. On her head the crown of twelve stars is a sign of the twelve months.

This understanding, of the importance of the calendar revealed to Enoch by Gabriel, is a key unlocking the events at the end of this age. For that reason this "sign" is given because from here on the events are directly tied to important days (appointed times) on that calendar.

Signs and appointed times were established at the beginning of life on earth to be revealed in our time!

11 The Day of the Living One

We now examine another key that can help us solve the puzzle of the end-time events. Moses received the Laws concerning the Feasts and High Days. These played an important role in history, although we know little about them. For example: the covenant between the tribes of Israel and Eyahuwah Elahim was made on the Feast of Weeks, which is also known as the Feast of Firstfruits. The one we know as Jesus, whose name in Hebrew, transliterated, is Eyahushuah, was crucified on Passover, the *fourteenth* day of the first month, not the fifteenth.

Some have heard about the Feast of Trumpets. The Day of Atonement is also known as Yom Kippur. Fewer, I think, have heard about the Feast of Tabernacles or Booths, the Last Great Day feast, and the Feast of Unleavened Bread. Along with the seven feasts are High or "Set-apart" days in which no work was to be done. These are the first and last days of the Feast of Unleavened Bread, the Feast of Weeks/Firstfruits, Feast of Trumpets, Day of Atonement, first day of the Feast of Tabernacles/Booths, and the Last Great Day Feast. Passover is a Feast day, but it is not a High day. You can look these up in the Torah, and in particular, in the book of Leviticus.

These, as we shall see, are linked forever to the calendar revealed to our father Enoch by Gabriel. Why was he given this calendar? I can guess that it was because at that time they went from day to day and from season to season without a reference to a calendar. Therefore, a calendar had to be revealed that would be in force through out all time or "until the new heavens and the new earth are created."

Enoch's calendar, as noted, has four quarters of exactly 13 weeks or 91 days. Each month has 30 days except the last month in each quarter, which has 31 days. The year has exactly 364 days. Of those days only 360 are counted for prophetic purposes. So three and one-half years is the same as 1260 days or

42 months. We simply ignore the last day in each quarter thus each month has 30 counted days. Quarters always start on solar events: the spring and fall equinoxes and the summer and winter solstices. Equinoxes are the two days in each year when the length of the day and night the same. In the northern hemisphere the summer solstice is the longest day, and winter solstice is the shortest day.

As noted, the year revealed to Enoch starts with the spring or vernal equinox, not some obscure day in the middle of winter. Also we now have an additional 1.242 days in our solar year. What do we do with it? Simply tack it on to the end of the year and not count it as a day of the week, and start the year at the equinox. Not counting days as a day of the weeks is similar to what other post-flood cultures did including Egypt. But Egypt put all 5 days at the end of the year, which defeats the purpose of the Revealed Calendar. The Revealed Calendar always starts on the fourth day of the week and so do the rest of the quarters. This means that the weekly Sabbath days always fall on the same days of the year, year after year. And so do the feasts and holy days. This is important when considering prophecy.

FEASTS, HIGH DAYS AND THE REVEALED CALENDAR

Here are the months and days on which the solar events, the feasts (or festivals) and high days come:

Month 1
- Day 1: Vernal or Spring Equinox: start of a new year; always the 4th day of the week.
- Day 4: First weekly Sabbath of the year. The 7th day of the week.
- Day 14: Passover: Not a high day and always the 3rd day of the week.
- Day 15: Feast of Unleavened Bread: high day; 4th day of the week; a 7-day feast
- Day 21: Last day of Unleavened Bread: high day; 3rd day of the week.

Month 3
- Day 15: Feast of Weeks and Firstfruits: high day; 1st day of the week.

Month 4
- Day 1: Summer Solstice

Month 7
- Day 1: Feast of Trumpets: high day; 4th day of the week; Fall equinox.
- Day 10: Day of Atonement: high day; 6th day of week.
- Day 15: Feast of Tabernacles: high day; 4th day of the week; a 7-day feast.
- Day 22: Last Great Day; high day; 4th day of the week; not part of Feast of Tabernacles.

Month 10:
- Day 1: Winter Solstice

These are known as the "set-apart" days. And if they were not kept on this time and on this calendar, they were considered as "polluted" and "unclean."

WHEN IS THE REAL SABBATH DAY?

The weekly Sabbath therefore would not come on our Saturday (Saturn's Day). Nor on Sunday (the Sun's Day) as the Christian religion would have it. These days come from Babylon. Because the Revealed Calendar always starts on the fourth day of the week, the *first weekly Sabbath day of the year would come three days later.*

From the prophet Malachi:

> Judah has acted treacherously, and an abomination has been done in Israel and in Jerusalem, for Judah has profaned that which has been set apart to Eyahuwah, which He had loved, and has married the daughter of a foreign mighty one [a god].

The marriage covenant between The Living One and Judah was ignored and counted as nothing. Judah returned from captivity in Babylon and brought back a new law, the Babylonian Talmud and the Babylonian lunar calendar. They were now "married to the daughter of Babylon." And spiritually they divorced the wife of "their youth," the one who was to be "your companion and the wife of your covenant." Zechariah, another post-exilic prophet, also confirms this message:

> "Oh, Zion! Escape you who dwell with the daughter of Babylon." From Zechariah 1.

This message is just as true today as it was then. This raises another question: **Whose job is it to determine the calendar and the Sabbaths? Is that** the job of a religion? Or does it belong to others?

It is an abomination that righteousness has been declared a "religious" thing. But the Torah, as given to Moses was not to be a foundation of a religion. The law was the responsibility of the rulers and the priests or Levites. No church, religious institution, or world-renown religious leader has the authority to make these determinations. These duties belong to the righteous rulers, kings, presidents who, with wisdom, understanding, and knowledge revealed by Elahim, are to establish the nation in a way that the people are blessed and know Eyahuwah – The Living One. The return and re-establishment of the clean, pure, and revealed calendar, on which the Feasts and High days of Eyahuwah Elahim can be kept as a blessing for the nations, is the duty of *kings and rulers*.

Along with them, the priests, as revealed in the law or Torah, are the ones who are the teachers, and not the rulers. The rest then is up to the people to live their lives in peace, love, and kindness:

> You shall love Eyahuwah your Elahim with all your heart,
> mind and strength, and your neighbor as yourself.

Malachi finished his prophecy with these revealed words that are just as true today as they were when he wrote in the Spirit of Eyahuwah:

> Remember the Torah of Moses, My servant, which I commanded him in Horeb for all Israel — laws and right-rulings.

Again Zechariah in the spirit says:

> "My wrath burns against the shepherds, and I lay charge
> against the leaders," declares Eyahuwah.

The shepherds, leaders of religions, lead the people astray, while the leaders, "the servants of all," run from their responsibilities.

SPIRITUAL TURMOIL IN HEAVEN AND EARTH

The end of the seventh age and the beginning of the eighth age is a time of great spiritual change. The evil rulers who now control the nations do not know the power of the spiritual forces behind their moves. As noted, Gabriel told Daniel the problems that Gabriel faced in the spiritual battle with the prince (another "angel") of Persia. He was alone until Michael came to help him. But he declared something that says how bad the situation really is:

> "There is no one supporting me against these [fallen spiritual princes], except Michael your prince!"

Then later Gabriel said,

> "Now at that time [the end of the seventh age] Michael shall stand up, the great prince who is standing over the sons of your people. And at that time there shall be a time of distress, such as never was since there was a nation, until that time."

It is that time when these days and events come together. To understand them we need the periods of time, the events, and the Revealed Calendar complete with the Feasts and High Days. Without these tools there can be no understanding.

THE DAY OF EYAHUWAH (HE WHO EXISTS)

The terminating event is the immediate transition from the first seven ages revealed to Enoch and the start of the eighth age. This is one day in the history of the world that is unlike any other, as Zechariah wrote (chapter 14):

> See! A day shall come for Eyahuwah, and your spoil shall be divided in your midst. And in that day His feet shall stand on the Mount of Olives, which faces Jerusalem on the east.
>
> And in that day it shall be: there is no light, it is dark. And it shall be one day which is known to Eyahuwah, neither day nor night, but at evening time [when the day ends] there shall be light. And Eyahuwah shall be King over all the earth. And in that day there shall be one Eyahuwah, and His Name one.
>
> And it shall be that all who are left from all the gentiles which came up against Jerusalem, shall go up from year to year to bow themselves to the King Eyahuwah of armies, and to observe the Festival of Tabernacles. And it shall be, that if anyone of the clans of the earth does not come up to Jerusalem to bow himself to the King, Eyahuwah of armies, on them there shall be no rain. ... This is the punishment of Egypt and the punishment of all the gentiles that do not come up to observe the Festival of Tabernacles.

At that time the observance of the Feasts and set-apart days, the equinoxes and solstices, and the restoration of Enoch's calendar will be a global change. There will not be different calendars, or calendars with private feasts and set-apart days according to practices of religious groups or sects.

> The earth will be full of the knowledge of Eyahuwah as the waters cover the sea. Isaiah 11:9

The final battle, between the Sons of Light and the Sons of Darkness, between the spiritual abominations who want to exalt themselves above Eyahuwah Elahim, and between the righteous and chosen and those who wish to destroy them, comes at the very end of the seventh age, and the victory starts at the beginning of the eighth age.

It is that last day that is the terminal day of these times:
> The end of the 2300 evenings and mornings
> The end of the time, times and half a time (three and a half years) when the beast and false prophet make war against the righteous and the elect.
> The end of the final "week" of Daniel's 70 weeks.
> The end of the first seven ages or "complete weeks" of Enoch's vision.

The next day starts a new age and a new year. The calendar revealed to Enoch starts at the same time the sun, moon and stars were set "for signs and appointed times, and for days and seasons." This is the 4th day of the week. Three days after that day the Sabbath was created.

Events leading up the Day

We saw above that the Festival or Feast of Tabernacles was going to be restored. Logically, then, the calendar that was created to map the Feasts and High Days ("the appointed times") will be restored also.

How do the other Feasts and High days fit into the picture? If we stipulate that this age ends at the end of the last year of this age on the Revealed Calendar of Enoch, as no other calendar lunar or solar, religious or political has any say in this matter, then what happened three and one half years earlier?

That would be the day of the Feast of Trumpets. Three and one half years counting backward from the first day of the first month is the Feast of Trumpets or "Shouting." Contrary to what many believe, rather than being a sound of war, it is considered to be a sound of prayer, shouting, trumpeting to Eyahuwah to rescue the people. It is also the time when the beast and false prophet begin to make war against the righteous and elect – the set-apart people. Also we can say that the day is also the same as when the two witnesses are given over to the power of the beast and false prophet and killed.

> "When the power of the holy people has been finally broken, all these things will be completed." [Note the future tense of that last phrase.] Daniel 12:7 NIV

And from Revelation 13:

> The beast was given a mouth to utter proud words and blasphemies and to exercise his authority for forty-two months. He opened his mouth to blaspheme Elah, and to slander his name and his dwelling place [lit. Tent or Tabernacle] and those who live in heaven. He was given power to make war against the set-apart ones and to conquer them. And he was given authority over every tribe, people, language and nation. All the inhabitants of the earth will worship the beast – all whose names have not been written in the book of life belonging to the Lamb that was slain from the creation of the world.
>
> He who has an ear, let him hear:
>
> If anyone goes into captivity, into captivity he will go. If anyone is to be killed with a sword, with a sword he will be killed.
>
> ***This calls for patient endurance and faithfulness on the part of the set-apart ones.***

For that reason, even though three and a half years of great trouble remain, the declaration is made:

> The kingdom of this world has become the kingdom of our Lord and of his Anointed One (Messiah or Chosen one), and he will reign for ever and ever. Revelation 11:15

SUMMARY OF THE LAST SEVEN YEARS

Using the Revealed Calendar, we can summarize the events at the end of this age: On the time of the new year, at the spring or vernal equinox, the two witnesses start their 42 week or three and a half years of prophesying to the people of the earth. This is also the start of the first year of the last seven years. During this time the sacrifices cease and the 2,300 evenings and mornings start a second day-by-day countdown to the end of the age. To calculate this you need to use sunset to sunset days, as the sacrifices were to be made every day and are therefore not affected by any calendar. This ceasing of sacrifices marks this day like a mile post on a highway. Then 1,290 days after this time counting on the Revealed Calendar, the abomination that leads to desolation is set up. This is described in Revelation 13 starting with verse 11.

Back to the two witnesses. *Three and a half years* later, when they have finish their prophesying, the beast is given the power over them and they are killed. Three and a half years from the start of work of the two witnesses is the Feast of Trumpets or Shouting. What really angers the beast is that three and one-half *days* after they are killed the two witnesses are raised up and they ascend to heaven. Now the beast determines to kill all the righteous and chosen ones. So he is given authority for *42 months*. From the Feast of Trumpets, the first day of the seventh month he starts to exercise his authority against the two witnesses and when he sees that killing them didn't work, he sets out to make war against the set-apart ones. At the end of that time Eyahuwah comes to the earth and crushes all the nations that tried to destroy Jerusalem and the people of Judah living there. These are the events for the last seven years of this age and includes the last two woes of Revelation.

The fact that Daniel and John use 1,260 days, three and one-half years ("times, time, and half a time"), and 42 months is a code to tell us which calendar to use. There is only one calendar where these time periods are the same and equal: the Revealed Calendar given to Enoch. Without that knowledge we could not determine the meaning of the 1,335 days

Waiting for the End of the 1,335 Days

One more period is left. As noted above there is a time of trouble that calls for "patient endurance and faithfulness on the part of the set-apart ones." This is a parallel statement about the 1,335 days — Daniel 12:13:

Blessed is he [or she] who is waiting earnestly and comes to the one thousand three hundred and thirty-five days.

This time period overlaps the two ages and at its end is the greatest event in the entire history of humanity to happen to the people and the rest of creation.

12 The 1,335th Day

What is the mysterious 1,335 day? Is it a day that ended a period of 1,335 years in the 1920s with the establishment of a new denomination or sect? Or does it have something to do with the six-day war of the Jews that ended in 1967. Or is it something that only God knows and that someday it will be revealed to the church or the Pope?

As we shall see it is none of those nor could it be. In order to comprehend the real truth about the 1,335 we must abandon all ideas that try to turn days into years and all traditional prophecies about which many wannabee prophets have written many books.

I sat down with a church minister before my Dad's funeral, and I mentioned in the conversation that the key to understanding prophecy is the Feasts and High days and their relationship to the Revealed Calendar. He looked at me and I could tell this puzzled him. Then he said, "Oh yes, we do need to spend some time on that."

Then later, a friend of mine came to my house and with him was a relative who was a Baptist Sunday school teacher, apparently from some big church somewhere. My friend was impressed with my book, and he wanted his relative to see me. The Sunday school teacher asked me, after looking at the book, "What is this book about?" I replied, "It is about the great event that will take place at the end of the 1,335 days." He put on the same puzzled expression as the minister and commented, "Oh yes, that is an important subject."

Neither of these had any knowledge about these things other than they had heard about the Feast Days and about the 1,335 days.

The last chapter ended with this statement given to Daniel which he wrote in chapter 12:

> "Blessed is he [or she] who is waiting earnestly and comes to the one thousand three hundred and thirty-five days."

Here is the shocking truth about when that day is and what it means for all creation. In the prior chapters I assembled all the tools, facts, and prophecies that led up to this very special day. It really is a day worth waiting for, but we must start now and not put it off. We must make that day and time the biggest target of our mental and spiritual focus, attention and energy.

But first a little review.

The last seven years of our age and beyond

All end-time events are tied to time periods and Feasts and High Days on the calendar revealed to our father Enoch. Without that revelation we cannot understand the important sequence of events of the end of our age.

There are three primary mile posts! These are not picked out of thin air. Instead, critical events happen at "appointed times" then we chart either backward or forward in time. The biggest marker is the Day of Eyahuwah, The Living One. The mile posts are:

The day when the two witnesses start their three and one half years prophecy. As noted, this starts on the spring equinox, which is the first day of the first month on the revealed calendar. We know this because of ...

The day when the two witnesses are killed by the beast [great nation or empire]. This is the fall equinox, which is first day of the seventh month on the revealed calendar. It is also the Feast of Trumpets or Shouting. We know this because three and one years afterward ...

The Day of The Living One comes as a day of deliverance that ends the three and one half year time of the beast's authority and power. This day is the first day of the first month and the spring equinox. It is also the first day of the eighth age.

There are also three other periods; one is independent of the Revealed Calendar and the other two are tied directly to it.

The day when the sacrifices cease. This starts a time of counting 2,300 evenings and mornings [days] independent of any calendar and continues until the Day of Eyahuwah.

The start of the 1,290 days period when the sacrifices cease. The end of the 1290 days is the day when the abomination is set up in the Set-apart city. This comes during the time

when the false prophet gives power to the beast sometime between the day the two witnesses are murdered and the Day of Eyahuwah.
- **The start of the 1,335 days**, which is a period related to a key event in the first list, but, as we shall see, it is tied to the last three and one half years. The 1,335 days is equal to three and one half years plus two and one half months. That means that it fits neatly into the end-time sequence of events.

SIGNS TIED TO ALL THE DESCENDENTS OF JACOB

The Feasts and the High days are appointed times and signs. These signs were to be closely associated with the 12 tribes of Jacob. They were spiritually married to Eyahuwah by a covenant. The people of all the tribes of Israel, not only the house of Judah, appears as a great and wondrous sign in heaven: "a woman clothed with the sun, with the moon under her feet, and a crown of twelve stars on her head." (Revelation 12)

Some say this was Mary. It is not. The sign included the woman, who is Israel, and the rest is a description of the relationship of the sun, moon and stars. The life of Israel, day after day, week after week, month after month, and year after year was "clothed" as noted, with perpetual events that started with the spring equinox that marked the new year on the 4th day of the week. Then three days later came the weekly Sabbath. Then came Passover, and so on. This was the clothing of the woman. Anyone who came to visit the people of Israel would have seen this garment covering all of Israel. And this would have marked Israel as a nation different from all other nations on earth. Also as noted, the calendar is solar, not lunar, in this vision of the woman, the moon is in a subordinate position, and the crown of stars are the twelve months, each with its own star or constellation.

Now, because the Pharisees imposed the Babylonian calendar on Judah, and the church put the Roman calendar on the other "lost" nations of Israel, the woman walks, naked and blind, in darkness carrying the moon on her back and no longer wearing the crown. But, this, too, will pass away and that is good news.

WHY KNOW ABOUT THIS SPECIAL TIME OF THE END?

Why would anyone want to know what will happen in the last several years of this age? I look at it as a blessing. Not everyone will understand these times, but those who are wise and have understanding will be aware that when they see these things, they will know that we are in the final "week" given to Daniel in the 70 weeks prophecy. If you know the truth now, then you know exactly what to look for. For that reason it is only revealed now – before that time comes on us. It will come shortly.

> If a ram's horn is blown in a city, do the people not tremble? If there is calamity in a city, shall not Eyahuwah have done it? ***For the Master, Eyahuwah, does no matter unless He reveals His secret to His servants the prophets.*** A lion has roared! Who is not afraid? The Master, Eyahuwah, has spoken! Who would not prophesy? Amos 3:6-8

A NEW TEMPLE OR TABERNACLE AND ALTAR IN JERUSALEM?

Another event with no calendar marker is the rebuilding of a partial temple or tabernacle structure with an altar on the "Temple Mount" in Jerusalem. It does not make sense that this would be a great structure like Solomon's or Herod's temple. After all this place is going to split in half when Eyahuwah's feet touch the Mount of Olives. (Zechariah 14) The building of a temple-like structure has no time period associated with it. But after it is built and is functioning, the real event to look for is when the two witnesses start to prophesy and three and a half years later they will be killed. So the start of the two witnesses prophecy is an event that starts on the first day of a new solar year on the spring equinox. From then on Enoch's Revealed Calendar tracks the events.

The next event is the cessation of the sacrifices. When this happens this starts the counting of the 2,300 evening and mornings before the beginning of the next age when the righteous are given authority to rule. Following the cessation of the daily sacrifices, will be the murder of the two witnesses in Jerusalem. This will happen, according to Revealed Calendar on the first day of the seventh month, which is the Feast of Trumpets and also the fall equinox. Three and one half *days* later, in view of the world, the two witnesses will be raised up and a voice will tell them to come up to heaven and they will ascend.

This is also the time when the counting of the 1,335 days starts. The Feast of Trumpets or "Shouting" is the time when the beast/dragon makes war against the righteous and the elect. This is NOT the time when Jesus returns as some believe. The trumpet shoutings are the strong cries and prayers of the descendants of Jacob to their Elahim to save them from this awful time and evil. It is a time of great spiritual battles and of great trouble on the earth. Three and a half years later the beast/dragon and those who joined with them take their war against Eyahuwah and his armies and are defeated. Also at this time the righteous and elect are raised from the dead.

Therefore, when the Day of Eyahuwah comes, three and a half years or 1,260 days of the 1,335 days have now passed and only 75 days remain.

What happens at the end of the 1,335 days?

There is only one interval of 1,335 days on the revealed calendar with the Feasts and Holy days applied to it. It starts at the time of the Feast of Trumpets. Then 1,260 days plus 75 days later brings us to the first Feast of Weeks, also called the Feast of Firstfruits, on the 15th day of third month of the first year of the next age! This is the only time period in these prophecies that spans both ages! This has been sealed until our day and time, and is now revealed to all who have ears that hear and eyes that see.

Why?

It is a sign and a message to the those who have wisdom and understanding. Those who hear and understand this message now have knowledge that can help them through this time of great tribulation that will come shortly upon the whole earth.

What is significant about that day?

It is a double Feast. It is the Feast of Weeks, and it is also the Feast of Firstfruits. Both reached their most significance at this time in the history of the human people.

The Feast of Weeks

This is a celebration of the first seven weeks of Enoch's vision. The Law instructs the people to "count" seven complete weeks starting with the week after the Feast of Unleavened Bread AND after the first weekly Sabbath *after* the Wave Sheaf was offered. Seven full weeks later ends with the weekly Sabbath, and the very next day, which is the first day of the week, is the Feast of Weeks and the Feast of Firstfruits. This is the 50th day and so some adopted the name as Pentecost. However, the original names are much more important. Thus the

Feast of Weeks signifies the completion of the first seven weeks or ages. The very next day, the day of this feast, also represents the start of the great Eighth age! The counting of the seven weeks is a memorial of the time of human rule and the keeping of this Feast and High day will allow the people and the nations to compare the past with the present right-ruling ages until the time of the new heavens and the new earth.

The Feast of Firstfruits

This Feast, which happens on the same day as the Feast of Weeks, is very unusual. *This is the day the entire creation has waited for.* It is the day when the righteous will be revealed to the world and presented before their Father in heaven. These are those who overcame *during the time of the first seven ages.* During this time they gained wisdom and understanding and separated themselves from the world and its unclean and crooked ways. Some came out of the Babylon religions. These are all the righteous from all nations, tribes and languages. In the Book of Revelation they are called the "innumerable multitude." Even though the greatest time of trouble in the world, even greater than the flood, happens at the end of this age, there has been a time of great tribulation or distress from the very beginning. It started with the trouble that Adam and Eve got into and the murder of their son, Abel, and it ends on the Day of Eyahuwah.

Before Christians get too comfortable in their fallacious hope of a "rapture" that they believe will "take them out of this time of trouble and guarantee their place in the Kingdom", think about this: the so-called "Church age" or "Age of Grace" is nothing less than the Age of Apostasy that Enoch saw in his vision. It is the seventh and last age before the great change to right-ruling. This means that all people around the earth who are engaged in religious activity need to deeply reconsider their current spiritual position, in other words, "repent and flee from the wrath to come." The proclamations by a Pope that "the only path to salvation is through the Catholic church" is not truth. It is a deception to lure people under their control. It is counter to salvation! The so-called "apostolic succession through Peter" is also false. The only succession is through Paul the Pharisee, who learned little to nothing from Peter.

Since Man walked this earth there has been only one way to salvation and this is righteousness, and that means right-doing that comes as a natural product of right-being, combined with wisdom, understanding and knowledge.

The Torah speaks of that Day

There are some details about this great event that we need to know. During the Feast of Unleavened Bread, on the first day of the week, a special event was to happen each year. A sheaf of wheat was presented to Elah as the Wave Sheaf. This was done by waving the sheaf in an overhead ascending motion. This symbolized the presenting of the Firstfruit or Firstborn of the harvest and is symbolic of the Firstborn Son raising from the dead and appearing before the Father. This is from Leviticus 23 and is part of what is to be done during the Feast of Unleavened Bread.

> And Eyahuwah spoke to Moses, saying, "Speak to the children of Israel, and you shall say to them, 'When you come into the land which I give you, and shall reap its harvest, then you shall bring a sheaf of the first-fruits of your harvest to the priest. And he shall wave the sheaf before Eyahuwah, for your acceptance. On the morrow [next day] after the Sabbath, the priest waves it.

Eyahushuah [Jesus] told Mary Magdalene in the garden on the "morrow after the Sabbath" after He had been raised from the dead:

> "Do not hold on to me, for I have not yet ascended to My Father. But go to my brothers and say to them, 'I am ascending to My Father and your Father, to My Elahim and your Elahim.'" John 20:17 The Scriptures

First understand that Eyahuwah ("He who exists") became Eyahushuah (("He who exists is the savior"). Eyahuwah is the One who made the covenants with our father's, including Enoch, Noah, Abraham, Isaac and Jacob. Eyahuwah came to the earth and was born, not in December, but during the Feast of Booths or Tabernacles after the 15th day of the seventh month on the revealed calendar. He is the One who spoke to Moses and to the descendants of Jacob at Mount Sinai. Then at the right time He came to His people to fulfill the terms and conditions of the covenants:

> And the Word became flesh and pitched his tent among us. John 1:14

The last part is a literal translation and is a reference to the Feast of Tabernacles [Tents] or Booths during which days He was born.

In this context let us now examine further what is written in the Torah in the book of Leviticus:

> And on that day when you wave the sheaf, you shall prepare a male lamb a year old, a perfect one, as a burnt offering to Eyahuwah, and its grain offering: two-tenths of an ephah of fine flour mixed with oil, and offering made by fire to Eyahuwah, a sweet fragrance, and its drink offering: one-fourth of a hin of wine. *And you do not eat bread of roasted grain or fresh grain until the same day that you have brought an offering to your Elahim — a law forever throughout your generations in all your dwelling.*

The offering of "bread of roasted grain or fresh grain" is not this offering, but one coming in the future as we shall see. Then it continues with the additional laws that tie the Feast of Unleavened Bread with the "seven weeks" and with the Feast of Firstfruits:

> And [starting] from the next day after the [weekly] Sabbath [which comes] after the day that you brought the sheaf of the wave offering, you shall count for yourselves seven complete Sabbaths [weeks].

In other words, the counting starts with the week that begins after the Sabbath that comes during the week when the wave sheaf is offered. The counting begins one week after the wave sheaf. That day is also the first day of the week and continues until seven full weeks have been counted.

> Until the morrow [next day] after the seventh Sabbath you count fifty days; then you shall bring a new grain offering to Eyahuwah.

It is this new grain offering that reveals why the day that ends the 1,335 days is one of the greatest days yet to happen in the history of humanity. There is only One assigned to make this a part of our life and that is Eyahuwah. From before there was a heaven and earth, He was Chosen to raise up Sons of Elah from the "stones" of the universe. The Firstfruits of that enormous project will be revealed on the Feast of Firstfruits at the end of the 1,335 days revealed to Daniel and sealed until this time.

Now let's see why this day is important?

13 The Fulfillment of Day 1,335

You now have the keys to understand the mystery of the 1335 days. These include the calendar revealed to Enoch, the Feasts and High days revealed to Moses, and the periods of time for the end-of-the-age events that were revealed to Daniel and to John. With this you can know the start and the end of the 1,335 days. Now learn why that day is so important!

THE 1,335 DAYS PROPHECY REVEALED

> For the Master, Eyahuwah, does no matter unless **He reveals His secre**t to His servants the prophets. Amos 3:7

The 1,335 day period begins with the death of the two-witnesses at the time when the beast was given power over the set-apart ones. He was given this power for the period that marks the last three and one half years of the seventh age, our age. Because of this great time of trouble, this becomes a time of waiting and patience while looking forward to the 1,335th day. The resurrection of the two-witnesses three and one half days after they were killed, offers hope to the righteous and the elect. The set-apart ones are encouraged to have patience during the last three and one half years, and to *wait for the day* that marks the end of the 1,335 day waiting period.

As noted, the death of the two-witnesses comes after a prior three and one half year period or 42 months during which they prophesied over the earth and its people. The day they were killed will be the same day as the Feast of Trumpets or Shouting, which is the first day of the seventh month on Enoch's calendar, and this is also the fall equinox. One thousand three hundred thirty five days from that High day takes us to another very important High Day on the 15th day of the third month during the first year of the eighth age. Enoch's year is counted as 360 days, regardless of how many actual days occur during a solar year. Therefore 1,335 days is equal to 360 + 360 + 360 +180 + 30 + 30 +15.

The final day of the 1,335 days occurs on the 15th day of the third month during the first year of the eighth age after the beast and false prophet are destroyed and the righteous and elect are raised up from the dead.

This High Day is the Feast of Weeks and the Feast of Firstfruits, a very special High Day. Some call this Pentecost. This High Day is linked to the Feast of Unleavened Bread, a seven day Feast that starts on the 15th day of the first month, which is always the fourth day of the week. During the Feast of Unleavened Bread, *on the first day of the week*, a Wave Sheaf offering is made, along with other sacrifices. Then from the day *after* the Sabbath of that same week, which is the first day of the week, the people were to count seven complete weeks. This symbolizes the completion of the first seven "weeks" or ages given to Enoch by a vision. The very next day, after the seven weeks are complete, is the 50th day. This is also the first day of the next week and the 15th day of the third month and the Feast of Weeks and the Feast of Firstfruits.

Now it is time to examine the events of that day as given to Moses in the Law or Torah. During the period of the seven weeks between the Feast of Unleavened Bread and the Feast of the Firstfruits, the people were instructed by the Law:

> And you do not eat bread or roasted grain or fresh grain until the same day that you have brought an offering to your Elahim — a law forever throughout all your generations in all your dwellings. Leviticus 23

In other words, this was a time when no harvest of grain was to be eaten. This is separate from the Feast of Unleavened Bread during which only unleavened bread was to be eaten, and that was for seven days. But during this time that lasted for seven completed Sabbaths no grain, neither roasted or new, was to be used in the making of bread for consumption. This says that during the seven weeks or ages of Enoch, there was to be no harvest of Firstfruits from among the people. But afterward another special offering was to be made to "your Elahim."

> Until the morrow after the seventh Sabbath, you count fifty days, *then you shall bring a new grain offering to Eyahuwah.* Bring from your dwellings for a Wave Offering two loaves of bread, of two tenths of an ephah of fine flour they are, baked with leaven, *Firstfruits* to Eyahuwah.

The Law describes other sacrifices for the day after the weekly Sabbath day during the Feast of Unleavened Bread. This is special first day of the week.

Yet even more sacrifices are required for the Feast of Firstfruits, also on the first day of the week after counting seven completed Sabbaths. None of the other Feast Days and High Days have even similar sacrificial duties.

On the first day of the week during the Feast of Unleavened Bread:

> And **on the day when you wave the sheaf**, you shall prepare a male lamb a year old, a perfect one, as a burnt offering to Eyahuwah, and its grain offering: two tenths of an ephah of fine flour mixed with oil, an offering made by fire to Eyahuwah, a sweet fragrance, and its drink offering of a hin of wine.

Now compare that with the offerings for the first day of the week that is the 15th day of the third month on the Feast of Firstfruits:

> **And beside the bread [the Wave Offering]**, you shall bring seven lambs a year old, perfect ones, and one young bull and two rams. They are a burnt offering to Eyahuwah, with their grain offering and their drink offering, an offering made by fire for a sweet fragrance to Eyahuwah. And you shall offer one male goat as a sin offering, and two male lambs a year old as a peace offering. And the priest shall wave them, beside the bread of the Firstfruits, as a wave offering before Eyahuwah, besides the two lambs. They are set apart to Eyahuwah for the priest.

If you were to evaluate the significance of a Feast and High day by the number and quality of the sacrifices made during that day, the Feast of Firstfruits ranks at the top!

As noted, the coming fulfillment of the Feast of Firstfruits is the greatest day in the history of the human race. At the start of eighth age, at the end of the 1,335 days which is the Feast of Firstfruits, **all who overcame the world during the prior seven ages of human life, will now come together, as the Wave Loaves, to ascend to Their Father and to Their Elahim, to be accepted into the Family, now as Sons of Elahim.**

Eyahuwah/Eyahushuah is the Firstfruit represented by the Wave Sheaf, and He was sacrificed before the foundation of the world. Then an innumerable mass of people from every tribe, language, and nation who washed their robes and made them white in the blood of the Lamb, are the Firstfruits, represented by the Wave Loaves. The mass of sacrifices is symbolic of the blood they shed and the sin they overcame, and of the greatness of Elahim who, *before the universe was created*, had been looking forward to THIS DAY!

THE TWO WAVE LOAVES

When the two wave loaves are made they start as one pile of bread dough made with leaven. Leaven is a symbol of sin. At the right time the one pile of dough is cut into two identical loaves. This is a symbol of Man being separated into two: a male and a female. This was not by taking a single "rib." The Hebrew literally means a "side." From Man came both man and woman, male and female. Man was made in the image and likeness of Elahim. After the resurrection to eternal life there is no sexual distinction. The new immortal body is neither male or female. Therefore, the two Wave Loaves represent man and woman both taken from Man, and now ascending to their Father and to their Family Elahim as individual and equal Sons of Elah.

This event is the BIG day for which we must cleanse ourselves and prepare, and having prepared, then we must earnestly wait for that day. The promise is not heaven or hell after we die. It is eternal life as a member of the Family of Elahim, after the resurrection from the dead. Those who fail to prepare and don't believe the prophecies of this great news can only look forward to a resurrection to a time of judgment during which time they will learn the knowledge of Eyahuwah. They will all be taught by Him! But they will have no part in the events at the end of the 1,335 days: The Feast celebrating the Firstfruits!

Here are some interesting insights to the Wave Sheaf and Loaves. The Wave Sheaf (Eyahuwah) is offered before the Seven Weeks [the world] begins:

> And if you call on the Father, who without partiality judges according to each one's work, pass the time of your sojourning in fear, knowing that you were redeemed [purchased] from your futile way of life inherited from your fathers, not with what is corruptible, silver and gold, but with the precious blood of Messiah, as of a lamb unblemished and spotless [perfect], *foreknown, indeed, before the foundation of the world, but manifested in these last times for your sakes,* who through Him believe in Elahim, who raised Him from the dead and gave Him esteem, so that your belief and expectation are in Elahim! I Peter 1:17-21

What this is saying, and is supported by other Scriptures, is that the plan created before the universe began included the atoning and redeeming sacrifice. Therefore, the sacrifice that took place on Passover and the symbolic Wave Sheaf offering made on the first day of the week during the Feast of Unleavened Bread, precedes the symbol of the first "seven weeks" of human existence! So during this time we can observe both the actual events combined with the symbols.

This also applies to the events leading up to the Feast of Weeks/Firstfruits. After the end of the period of the "seven weeks", a new age is established and the rule over the earth and its people is given to the righteous, those who overcame the world during the first seven weeks or ages. The overcomers are presented to their Father and their Elahim [Family] at the Feast of Firstfruits. They all died not having received what was promised and they trusted Elahim to raise them from grave. They, like their Brother, the Living One who died but is alive forever, gained the right to be called the Sons of Elah, only this time on the actual fulfillment day: the Feast of Firstfruits, which is the end of the 1,335 days!

While writing this I have been pouring over the book of Hebrews [IBRIM] because this understanding is its main subject. Here is just a sample from The Scriptures translation:

> For it was fitting for Him, because of Whom all are and through Whom all are, in bringing MANY SONS to esteem, to make the Princely Leader of their deliverance perfect through sufferings. For both He who sets apart and those who are set-apart are all of One [FAMILY (NIV)], for which reason He is not ashamed to call them BROTHERS, saying, "I shall announce Your Name to My brothers, in the midst of the congregation I shall sing praise to You."
>
> Therefore, since the children share in flesh and blood, He Himself shared in the same, so that by means of His death He might destroy him having the power of death, that is, the devil, and deliver those who throughout their life were held in slavery by fear death. For, doubtless, He does not take hold of messengers [angels], but He does take hold of the seed of Abraham!
>
> So in every way He had to be made like His brothers, in or-

der to become a compassionate and trustworthy High Priest in matters relating to Elahim, to make atonement for the sins of the people. For in what He had suffered, Himself being tried, He is able to help those who are tried.

And as it awaits men to die once, and after this the judgment, so also the Messiah, having been offered to bear the sins of many, shall appear a second time, apart from sin, *to those **waiting** for Him, unto deliverance.*

The cry of the people rings out to Elahim at the time of the death of the two witnesses, who had been their help for three and one half years. The two-witnesses are raised up by Elahim after three and one half days to encourage the people who believed! Now the time of patience and waiting also begins until the return of Eyahuwah/Eyahushuah who delivers his people on the first day of the first year of that age and raises them ALL from the dead. Seventy five days later, the waiting comes to an end at the Feast of Firstfruits, when the righteous ascend to their Father and their Elahim [Family].

The rest of people on earth look on feeling both sadness and mourning mixed with hope that at some time in the future they will be added to the highly esteemed Family of Elah: Elahim.

What you have read is the true meaning of the 1,335 days. It is no longer sealed! We are now at the time in the history of humanity when these things will shortly come to pass. It is time now to prepare and get ready. It is a time to make straight paths for our feet.

Now lets take another glimpse at the world of the future.

III

"Behold, My Beloved!"

Prepare for the Future

Then shall those who fear Eyahuwah [He who exists] speak to one another, and Eyahuwah listen and hear, and a book of remembrance be written before Him, of those who fear Eyahuwah, and those who think upon His Name.

"And they shall be Mine," said Eyahuwah of hosts, "on that day that I prepare a treasured possession. And I shall spare them as a man spares a son who serves him."

Then you shall again see the difference between the righteous and the wrong, between one who serves Elahim, and one who does not serve Him. Malachi 3:16-18

Then the survivors from all the nations that have attacked Jerusalem will go up year after year to worship the King, Eyahuwah Almighty, and *to celebrate the Feast of Tabernacles*. If any of the peoples of the earth do not go up to Jerusalem to worship the King, Eyahuwah Almighty, they will have no rain. If the Egyptian people do not go up and take part, they will have no rain. Eyahuwah will bring upon them the plague he inflicts on the nations that do not go up to celebrate the Feast of Tabernacles. This will be the punishment of Egypt and the punishment of all the nations that do not go up to celebrate the Feast of Tabernacles.
Zechariah 14:16-19

Do not think that I have come to abolish the Law and the Prophets. I have not come to abolish them, but to keep them. I tell you the truth, until heaven and earth disappear, not the smallest letter, not the least stroke of a pen will by any means disappear from the Law until everything is accomplished.
Matthew 5:17-18

14 "In the Image of God"

"Dear friends, now we are the children of God, and *what we shall be **has not yet** been made known.*" (I John 3:2)

Prophecy does not require our belief. If there are true prophecies, they will be fulfilled whether or not we believe or even know about them. So it will be with the fulfillment of the destiny of the human race. The Apostle John wrote something often missed by the readers. In the first chapter, John gives a clue to one of the greatest mysteries revealed to the apostles and disciples:

"As many as received Him (Eyahushuah), to them He gave *the right to become offspring of God** (Elah), even to those who believe in His name ('He who exists delivers us'), who are born [actually, "begotten" or conceived], not of blood, nor of the will [desire] of the flesh, nor of the will [desire] of man, but of God (Elah)."

*The Greek word *Theos* when translated into Hebrew becomes either *Elah* or *Elahim*.

From the very beginning the desire or will of Elahim has always been "Let US make Man in OUR image and after OUR likeness." Elahim, from before the beginning, focused on adding to the population of his domain by giving birth to offspring. In other scriptures these beings are called "The Sons of God" and "The Sons of Man."

This is not a sexist thing. Nor does it in any way imply that only males of the species are allowed – like some exclusive club. In the Domain or Kingdom of Elahim there is neither a male being nor a female being. So the *Offspring of God* are neither men nor women. They are called "Sons" , "Offspring" or "Children."

John's verse above tells the good news of the conceiving or begetting. The process of birthing the Sons of God requires both a Father and a Mother and the conception takes place in the Bridal Chamber. These are images, but have great importance for us. In fact, the Bridal Chamber was one of the most important "sacraments" of the real Christians, and is described in the *Gospel of Philip*.

Conception is one thing. Birth is another. The verses above talk about the conception. The verses in John 3 talk about the birth:

> "Truly, truly, I say to you, unless one is born of water *and* the Spirit, (that one) cannot enter the Kingdom of Elahim. That which is born of the flesh is flesh and that which is born of the Spirit is spirit."

If you are reading this, you are born of water and of the flesh. Spiritually speaking the fleshy process is an image of the spiritual. Both require conception by the Father. Then the job of giving birth belongs to the Mother.

But who is the Mother?

The Mother nourishes us, protects us, comforts us. She feeds us milk from her body. As we grow she feeds us bread and meat. She teaches us all things including things that we must know about our future and what is happening around us. She teaches us about our Father. She cares for us – until the time we have matured into what were destined to become. But even then she is still our Mother and this care never ceases.

This was true of my mother who died on December 23, 2005. But her life also is an image. Throughout her life her strongest desire was to do the will of God and she submitted herself to that, even though she, for most of her life, did not know just what God's will was. But after she died my brothers and I realized that she did God's will: She was a great mother.

The Greek word translated Spirit is "pneuma", from which we get the word pneumonia. It is translated wind, breath, or spirit. In Hebrew the word "ruach" is translated wind, breath or spirit. If the Greek "pneuma" is translated to Hebrew, "ruach" is the word that is used.

So what is the difference? The gender differs. The Greek word is neuter. The Hebrew word is feminine as is the Aramaic (rukha). That the word is neuter in Greek is not important. We simply must deal with it. But that the word is feminine in Hebrew and Aramaic is far more important. At least it was to the Apostles and Disciples.

In the *Gospel of Thomas*,

Eyahushuah says, "For my mother bore me, yet my true Mother gave me the Life."

Who, then, is the true Mother? The One who gives the Life.:

Again Eyahushuah says in John 6:63, "The Spirit gives Life; the flesh counts for nothing."

The true Mother is the Holy "Spirit of Truth that goes out from the Father" – as Eve came out of Man. She, the Spirit, is the *parakletos* – the One who is our helper, encourager, comforter, advocate, intercessor, and counselor: our true Mother! (John 15,16)

Now we know what we shall be

So Elahim created Man in His own image, in the image of Elahim created He him. Genesis 1:27

The statement "Let US make Man in OUR image and after OUR likeness" implies that Man was made androgynous. Androgynous is made from two Greek root words: andros or "man" and gynos or "woman." Androgynous means having the characteristics of both man and woman. Because the likeness of Elahim is androgynous, the Beings in Elahim "neither marry nor are given in marriage."

All that exists came out from a single Source. From the One in the Hebrew Scriptures called "El" or "Elah" came everything.

The word אל "El" is most often connected with other words that show that El is part of or the cause of some action. When used by itself another letter is added making אלה the pronunciation "Elah" {ehl-ah}, meaning "God, the Self, the All." In other words, there is nothing but Elah and all else is a manifestation or creation of Elah.

Other ancient documents show that the people believed that Elah meditated upon himself and brought forth as a manifestation of his meditations all that exists including all other beings, the universe and all its powers, and all life both physical and spiritual. All that exists therefore is the product of Elah expressing himself as creation.

In Hebraic geometry the perfect hexagon, with six equal sides, is a symbol of Elah. Each day of creation then becomes another hexagon, another manifestation of Elah. When the six days were finished, a seventh day naturally came into existence. Not by work, but by doing nothing! Six equal and perfect hexagons, when placed together in a circle, form another hexagon in the center of equal size and perfection.

Within Elah are both male and female. If we take a single hexagon and join three corners, we can produce two equilateral triangles: one with a point up (male) and the other with a point down (female). Some call this the "Star of David". When the two triangles join they produce another hexagon in the center. The union of the male and female in Elah creates the entity.

But this new creation, this Son of Elah, contains the same power and perfection to produce other Sons of Elah. From the One came "Elahs" or Elahim (אלהים). *Elah* in Hebrew is the masculine singular form for the One. *Elahim* is the masculine plural for the Domain or Kingdom of Elahim that contains the Sons of Elah.

Elahim literally means "Mighty Ones" and the home of the "Might Ones". There is oneness is Elahim and when Elahim speaks, it speaks as One Family. Eyahuwah represents Elahim and is often called "Eyahuwah Elahim" in the Scriptures. If some person is called a "Man of God," that person is a Man of Elahim — a person whose life comes from a connection with all the powers of Elahim. Eliyahu (Elijah) and Enoch were such men.

We have all been led to believe that Adam gave up a "rib" when Eve was created. But that is not true to the Hebrew. In only two places is the Hebrew word צלע "tzehlag" translated "rib". They are both in Genesis 2. Most often the word is translated "side, side chamber, boards or planks". Also it is a feminine word like "ruach" or spirit. The Ancient Hebrew letter of the first letter of this word is a pictograph of the right side of a man who is lying down: ༽

Everett Fox in *The Five Books of Moses* adds a footnote to this passage to say that the translation of *tzehlag* to sides parallels "other ancient peoples' concept of an original being that was androgynous."

Elahim created *androgynous* Man in the image of Elahim. Then from Man came both male and female. From Man, *Eyahuwah* took *the female side* and the male side remained to produce the matched set. So from Man was taken the side that was feminine. Eve was made female and Adam was then made male – at the same time! Like two loaves of bread made from one batch of dough, so Adam and Eve came into being by dividing Man into two. From this we have the image of the Wave Loaves Offering made by dividing one batch of dough made with leaven. So both Adam and Eve can be considered "Sons" of Man.

> He created *them* Male *and* Female. Genesis 1:27

Nowhere does the Scripture indicate that Man the human was first made male! Although, the languages use masculine pronouns in reference to Man. Because Man was made in the image and likeness of Elahim, one could not tell whether Man was male or female. The result was Adam, the male part of Man, and Eve, the female taken from Man. And Adam became the father and Eve the mother of the Sons of Man.

Mary's Conception: How it Happened.

Now when Eyahushuah was conceived he had a "father" and mother of the flesh and a Father and Mother in the Spirit. Before this time, the One who became the Father was called the "Lord of Spirits" (1 Enoch). From the Lord of Spirits came both male and female. From the Lord of Spirits was taken one "side" – the female side, she was called the Holy Spirit who became the Mother of the Sons of God. The male side of Lord of Spirits became the Father of the Sons of God. Man was indeed made in the image of Elahim.

When Mary was told the news about her becoming pregnant and giving birth, she asked, "How will this be since I am a virgin?"

And the messenger (angel) told her how:

"The Holy Spirit will come upon you *and* the Power of the
Most High will overshadow you."

The Holy Spirit did not impregnate Mary (Gospel of Philip 18), as people mistakenly believe. The union took place in the *spiritual Bridal Chamber*, between the Bridegroom, the Most High One, who became the Father, and the Bride, the Holy Spirit, who became the Mother. Mary was filled with the Holy Spirit. Then the Power of the Most High brought about the conception of the Son of Man who would become the firstborn Son of God.

"So the holy one to be born will be called the Son of God"
(Luke 1:34:35).

The Lord of Spirits become the Father, whose only begotten Son was Jesus or, more correctly, Eyahushuah. Jesus also became the Firstborn of many Brothers, because from that time on more children were conceived by the will of the Father and given Life by the Holy Spirit, the *parakletos*, the Mother of all Life.

Note the language of Acts 1:8, "But you will receive power when the Holy Spirit comes on you." Mary was "baptized or immersed in the Holy Spirit when the Holy Spirit (She) came on her" and then the union with the Power of the

Most High (The "Lord of Spirits") caused Mary to conceive.

As you read these scriptures, keep in mind that the apostles and disciples were thinking about the Hebrew/Aramaic feminine Spirit (ruach/rukha). They were not thinking of the Greek neuter word pneuma. Many translators erred when they mistranslated the neuter Greek (pneuma) to English and assumed a masculine gender. As a result the church doggedly holds on to the notion that a "Trinity" consists of three masculine entities. But the Scriptures show that there is a Father and a Mother, and many Sons! Eyahushuah was only the first of many! The Apostles and disciples knew about the Father (Lord of Spirits), the Mother (Holy Spirit) and the Son (Eyahuwah/Eyahushuah).

The Birth of the Sons of Elah

The greatest event yet to happen to the human kind is the transformation by the birthing process of the resurrection to become the Sons of Elah: All creation waits for this.

> Eyahushuah said, "The people of this age marry and are given in marriage. But those who are considered worthy of taking part in that age and in the resurrection from the dead will neither marry nor be given in marriage, and they can no longer die; for they are like the angels. [Messengers].
>
> They are Elah's children because they are children of the resurrection. ... Elah is not the Elah of the dead, but of the living, for to Elah all are alive." Luke 20:34-38

The Sons of Elah will be presented before their Father on the Feast of the Firstfruits on the 15th day of the third month of the Prophetic Calendar in the 8th "Week" or Age. This event will continue to happen and more offspring of Man will grow and change and become transformed into Sons of Elah by this powerful conception and birthing process! This is the gospel the world should be hearing, instead of a message of condemnation and threat, if one does not join with some religion.

15 "We Shall Be Like Him"

There are no direct statements in that Scriptures say, "This is what you will be like." But, we can get a very good picture by looking at our "Brother." There is much confusion about who the one we call "Jesus" really was and what he did. Some say he was "a great teacher." I guess that gets them off the hook and they can get on with whatever it is they do. Others say he was a man, like Buddha. And some believe he was God.

He asked his disciples, "Who do you say I am?" They answered, "You are the Christ, *the Son of the Living God*." We will get back to this answer later.

Jesus asked the Pharisees, "What do you think about the *Messiah* (Hebrew for Christ)? Whose son is he?" They answered, "The son of David."

This is a currently held position by the Jews, but Jesus, whose name is really Eyahushuah, said to them, "How is it that David, speaking by the Spirit, calls him 'Lord'? For he says, "Eyahuwah said to *my* Lord: "Sit at my right hand until I put your enemies under your feet." ' If then David calls him 'Lord,' how can he be his son?"

They could not answer him and never asked him another question. The reference is to Psalm 110, which was a point of confusion then and still is today. Who is this mysterious Lord referred to here? This same confusion exists with Isaiah 52 and 53. Who is the servant who was to suffer and the one Eyahuwah "has laid upon the iniquity of us all?" Is this some form of insane cruelty? Or is this justice in its highest form – beyond even our ability to imagine?

Both David and Isaiah were "speaking by the spirit" when they wrote these words. So the answers must come also from the spirit – something that usually is not part of scholarly research.

"He who exists" or "The Living One" That is the Name

The one we call Lord has a name and the use of the word "Lord" is only done to hide the name. "Lord" is really the meaning of the word "Baal" (Bah-al), which also means "Overseer" or "Overlord" or "Master". The Jews also use the word "ha-shem", which means "The Name" so that they can avoid saying the Name. And in prayers they use "Adonai" in place of יהוה. But "Lord" does not translate the real meaning of the Hebrew יהוה. Instead it is a substitute to avoid both translation and transliteration.

Some conclude that the real pronunciation is unknown. Or is it? Here is what "the Lord" says:

> "And all day long my name is constantly blasphemed.
> Therefore my People will know my name; therefore in that
> day they will know that it is I who foretold it. Yes, it is I." Isaiah
> 52:5-6.

And in another place speaking in spirit to the People of all the Nations of Israel as though Israel is a wife:

> "In that day," declares יהוה, "you will call me 'my hus-
> band'; you will no longer call me 'my master' [Lord or literal-
> ly 'Baali']. I will remove the names of the Baals from her lips;
> no longer will their names be invoked." Hosea 2:17-18 NIV.

Even today throughout both the Christian and Jewish religions, the name "יהוה" is referred to as "Lord." But what is the real name? It is "He who Exists," which can also mean "The Living One."

> Beginning from the premise that the Tetragrammaton let-
> ters (יהוה) *were not converted to vowels* but *were always three
> long vowels*, the original full pronunciation can be unequivo-
> cally given as EYAHUWAH. (Leet)

The Hebrew pronunciation of the English name "Elijah" provides further evidence: In Hebrew it is pronounced EL - EYAHU. The last three letters are the long vowels sounds יהו. They are the vowels of the Tetragrammaton. And as I wrote earlier, the People of Judah can be called the People of Eyahudah or Eyahudim. The name contains the three long vowels יהו.

That is fine, as far as pronunciation goes. But far more important is the character of the One to whom this name belongs. He was *created* before the universe. He was given a name through which He was known in the domain of Elahim and to the offspring of Man. He is the One who exists! In contrast to others created by human thought, He is the only One who truly exists. He is the One who gave promises to our fathers, and because He exists He will carry out and do what He promised He would. He can do that because He exists. He also has the power and can give power and authority to anyone He desires, yet without losing anything, because He says, "I am with you always."

At one time He was dead: "I am the Living One, and I become dead, but see, I am living forever and ever. This is true. And I possess the keys of the grave and of death." (Rev. 1) Because He exists, every person has hope, whether alive or in the grave.

Mystical Resources

Discovering knowledge of both science and the spiritual requires true mystical exploration. The apostles gave it the name *repose* (Shabbat) or *the rest of contemplation*. Freedom from anxiety, worry, fear, strain and exertion by entering into restful contemplation opens up a spiritual connection – the Elahim Connection. Repose or Shabbat Rest becomes the portal into the spiritual and opens the way to knowledge, understanding and wisdom.

> Unless you fast from the system, you shall not find the Kingdom {of Elahim}. Unless you keep the entire week as Sabbath, you shall not behold the Father.
> (Metalogos, Gospel of Thomas 27).

Fasting from the system indicates a willingness to not depend upon the system or the world for your life. Your real life, here and now, depends upon the Kingdom of Elahim from which you have received Life.

And regarding keeping the Sabbath Rest for the entire week indicates a way of life, and not the keeping of a single day in the week. This does not imply laziness. On the contrary, the person who keeps this rest can be even more creative and more productive than those who do not, including those who attempt to keep the Sabbath day even though on an unclean day.

The entering into His rest, this perpetual Sabbath, puts one in a relationship where all the resources of the Kingdom of Elahim work in concert in the life of the individual. So as opportunities are presented, benefits can abound. It is the Spirit that draws upon the Resources of Elahim to assist and aid those who live in this Repose or Rest. And Ministering Spirits are "sent to serve those who will inherit salvation." (Hebrews 1:14).

The Sons of the Kingdom of Elahim enter into the Eternal Life now, though in a perishable body. So death becomes a type of sleep, and when they awake, they awake with an immortal body. All those who will become the Sons of the

Kingdom must first be born of the flesh and live in the flesh and then die and be born again by the resurrection.

But after Eyahushuah comes to the earth future Sons of the Kingdom, not resurrected to Life at his return, but instead resurrected to judgment will live out their lives in the flesh and, at the right time, be changed. Each year at that day when the Feast of Firstfruits comes, people as "Wave Loaves" will come from "wherever they live" to be presented before their Father.

Raised to Reality and Awareness

The resurrection to "judgment and eternal abhorrence" is not a resurrection to condemnation. It is rather a resurrection to *realization and awareness*. Those who awake will become aware of the way they lived their life before. They will realize the profound difference between life by the flesh and Life by the Spirit. And they will abhor and condemn their own blindness and weakness and will praise their Father and the firstborn Son and his Brothers. When they are immersed into the Holy Spirit, they will become unborn Sons of God, begotten by the Father, and they will receive Life from their Mother, the Holy Spirit. When they are ready, they will be born and be presented before the Father, just as a newborn infant is presented to the father at birth.

All of us, at sometime in our life must be immersed into the Spirit and, when we are born of the Spirit, be presented before the Father to be recognized as a true Son of God. The "end of the 1335 days" is the first time in the history of humanity when the Sons will be presented before the Father!

This is really the essence of our *Lifetime* and our reason for being alive!

Some may ask, "Why have we not heard this from our church or synagogue?" The church's goal is to proselytize and teach their dogma. That means they spend much effort "to induce someone to join their faith." This they mistakenly call "evangelization." Christians want to convert anybody and everybody. And every new proselyte seems to confirm to the other proselytes that they must be on the right track, otherwise, why would someone want to join with them? They measure success by numbers of proselytes. The Christians have even gone so far as to say that they are "true Jews in the spirit."

On the other hand, Jews study their writings and perform their traditions. If someone desires to join with them, he can and in doing so becomes a novice and must begin a process of learning. I have little personal experience with the Jewish religion and not even one of my many Jewish friends tried to proselytize me.

The apostles did not proselytize. They taught. They proclaimed "good news," not a message of condemnation if the hearers did not accept the message. Preaching or proclaiming the good news regardless of the outcome was their objective. This was true evangelization. The phonetic Greek for "good message (news)" is *euangelos*: eu = good, angelos = message. An "angel" is a "messenger." An "evangelist" is a messenger of good. If the hearers of this good news ignore or disbelieve the message, then fine, the messenger goes on to the next. But trying to "induce others to join their faith" was never part of their objective or practice. And when you understand the good news as presented in this book, you will understand why.

MESSAGE TO THE CHURCHES:

For the churches the time has come for them to open their eyes to the good news that was at first delivered by the Apostles, and to turn from preaching a message of condemnation. The time is at hand for those who call themselves by the name of the Chosen One to wash their robes and make them white. It is time for them to take a good look at their own state and not worry about those they call the "lost" – as if God is off somewhere hunting or perhaps, sleeping on the job. They need to turn away from the idea that the "church" is where all the "riches" of truth are kept and that they are "wealthy and do not need anything because they 'have the church'":

> You say, "I am rich; I have acquired wealth and do not need a thing. But you do not realize that you are wretched, pitiful, poor, blind and naked. I counsel you to buy from me gold refined in the fire, so you can become rich; and white clothes to wear, so you can cover your shameful nakedness; and salve to put on your eyes, so you can see. Those whom I love I rebuke and discipline. So be earnest and repent."
> Revelation 3:17-19.

If the Church and its proselytes do not turn from this apostasy, then after the resurrection, they will find themselves on the outside where there is "weeping and gnashing of teeth." Then they will fall down at the feet of the Sons of Elah and acknowledge that the one they call "Jesus", whose name is Eyahushuah, loved those who loved the truth.

Message to Judah:

And to Judah, who rejected יהוה when he declared, "A body you have prepared for me" and "I have come to do your will, O, Elahim." You allowed yourself to be blinded by the foolishness and proselytizing of the Christian religions that were born out of apostasy rather than truth. The one they call "Jesus" is actually the one you will not name. Jesus' real name is "יהוה our Savior". And he came to fulfill the Law – not do away with it. Here's how:

The People of Israel made the covenant of life or death with יהוה when they received the tablets of stone and the Law. But they did not keep the covenant and brought death upon themselves and their children. And because the People of Israel were destined to become Sons of God and Kings and Priests, יהוה came in the flesh, and became a faithful servant to offer Himself as a sacrifice and to purchase a People with His own body and blood. He fulfilled the requirements of both the Law and the other covenants, like the covenant made with David: It was יהוה *in the flesh* who received the "beatings with rods" promised to David's offspring on account of their wrong doing.

So on one hand as Eyahuwah, he covenanted with the People and with David, and on the other as Eyahushuah he fulfilled the Law and Covenants by taking the promised punishment upon Himself. So the Law was fulfilled by His death. By these acts He bought their debt. And by His resurrection, the Son of Man, returned to His Father, now as the Son of God.

Prophecy says "יהוה is Coming to Earth"

יהוה, the One who made the Covenants with our fathers, will return to save the world starting with Judah and the house of David. But this is not the first time He came to earth. The first time He came as the One who made a sacrifice of his physical body to pay our debt to the Law and in accordance with the Covenants. Now who is it that promised to come to the earth to "save" us from our enemies at the end of the age? Was it not יהוה?

> Lo, a day of יהוה is coming when your spoil shall be divided in your midst! For I will gather all the nations to Jerusalem for war: The city shall be captured, the houses plundered; and the woman violated; and a part of the city shall go into exile. But the rest of the population shall not be uprooted from the city.

> Then יהוה will come forth and make war on those nations, as He is wont to make war on a day of battle. On that day, He will set His feet on the Mount of Olives, near Jerusalem on the east; and the Mount of Olives shall split across from east to west....
>
> And יהוה אלהים, with all the holy beings, will come to you.
>
> ... And יהוה *shall be **King** over all the earth*; in that day there shall be one יהוה with *one* name. ...
>
> All who survive of all those nations that came up against Jerusalem shall make a pilgrimage year by year to bow low to the **King** יהוה of Hosts [Armies] and to observe the Feast of Booths [Tabernacles]. ...
>
> In that day, even the bells on the horses shall be inscribed "Holy to יהוה." The metal pots in the House of יהוה shall be like the basins before the altar; indeed every metal pot in Jerusalem and Judah shall be holy to יהוה of Hosts. (Zechariah 14, JSB)

Now how could "King יהוה" be King over all the earth if he was not also a descendant of David? How could the one Christians call "Jesus" fulfill this promised and prophesied return, if he was not also יהוה who came in the flesh? How could Jesus be named the one who will "Save the People from their sins" when it was יהוה who said in the Spirit,

> "I am יהוה אלהים who brought you out of Egypt. You shall acknowledge no אלהים but me, **no Savior except me.**" Hosea 13:4

And again:

> Return, O Israel to יהוה אלהים. Your sins have been your downfall! Take words with you and return to יהוה. Say to Him: "Forgive all our sins and receive us graciously, that we may offer the fruit of our lips." Hosea 14:1,2

And again in Zechariah is another passage where יהוה talks about Himself in the third person as He did in Isaiah 52 and 53 and in Psalm 110:

> "And it will come about **in that day** that I [יהוה] will set about to destroy all the nations that come against Jerusalem. And I will pour out on the house of David and on the inhabit-

ants of Jerusalem, the Spirit of grace and of supplication, so that **they will look on *Me* whom they have pierced**; and **they will mourn for *Him***, as one mourns for an only son, and they will weep bitterly over Him, like the bitter weeping over a first-born." Zechariah 12:9-10 NIV

"*They will look on ME ... and ... mourn for HIM.*"

Amazing!

And believe it or not, this will be the message preached at the first Passover of the new age. Then immediately following Passover will come the first Days of Unleavened Bread in the new age, where the people will learn to eat the unleavened bread of Truth and not the polluted and unclean bread of their former religions. Then the earth will start filling up with the knowledge of יהוה "as the waters cover the earth."

Enoch also saw visions of this special being:

> And I asked the [messenger] who went with me and showed me all the hidden things, concerning that Son of Man, who he was, and whence he was, (and) why he went with the Head of Days. And he answered and said to me:
>
> "This is the Son of Man who has righteousness, with whom dwells righteousness, and who reveals all the treasures of that which is hidden, because the Lord of Spirits has chosen him, and whose lot has the pre-eminence before the Lord of Spirits in uprightness for ever. And *this Son of Man* whom you have seen *shall put down the kings and the mighty from their seats, and the strong from their thrones, and shall loosen the reins of the strong, and break the teeth of the sinners.*" Enoch 46:2-4
>
> And [it was] at that hour that *the Son of Man was named* in the presence of the Lord of Spirits, and his name before the Head of Days. Yes, **before the sun and the signs were created, before the stars of heaven were made**, his name was named before the Lord of Spirits. He shall be a staff to the righteous whereon to stay themselves and not fall, and he shall be a light to the Gentiles, and hope to those who are troubled of heart.
>
> *All who dwell on earth shall fall down and worship before him, and will praise and bless and celebrate with song the*

Lord of Spirits.

For this reason has he been chosen and hidden before Him, before the creation of the world and for evermore. And the wisdom of the Lord of Spirits has revealed him to the holy and righteous; for he has preserved the lot of the righteous ... **For in his name, they are saved.**
Enoch 48:2-7

Sacrifice and offering you did not desire, but a body you prepared for *Me*; with burnt offerings and sin offerings you were not pleased. [Although the Law required them to be made.] Then said I, "Here *I am* — it is written about *Me* in the scroll — I have come to do your will, O Elah. Psalm 40, [Sept].

He is the One who was chosen before the universe was created to be a Son of Man, to be born of the flesh, so that He could become a Son of God, born of the Spirit by the resurrection from the dead. His name is EYAHUWAH! *He exists!* He is of the Family of [אלהים] Elahim. And He is the *Firstborn* of many Brothers.

In bringing many Sons to glory, it was fitting that God [Elahim], for whom and through whom everything exists, should make the Author and Leader of their salvation perfect through suffering. Both the One who makes men holy and those who are made holy are *of the same Family.* So Eyahushuah is not ashamed to call them Brothers! Hebrews 2:10 NIV

EYAHUWAH and EYAHUSHUAH are the names of One Being: The One who was Chosen before the universe was created. He is the Son of Man who became the Son of God, by becoming flesh, paying our debts to the Law and Covenants, and being raised from the dead, He returned to his Father. He is the One who exists and who is coming back as our *only* Savior!

"Blessed is the one who waits for and reaches the end of the 1335 days." Daniel 12:12

"Everyone who has this hope in him purifies himself, just as He is pure." I John 3:3

> What is Man that you are mindful of him, the Son of Man that you care for him? You made him [for a little while] lower than Elahim and crowned him with glory and honor. You made him ruler over the works of your hands; You put everything under his feet. Psalm 8:4-6

> The Chosen One is faithful as a son over Elah's house. And WE are His House, if we hold on to our courage and the hope of which we boast. Hebrews 3:6

> And when I turned I saw ... one like a Son of Man, dressed in a robe reaching down to his feet and with a golden sash around his chest. His head and his hair were white like wool, as white as snow, and his eyes were like blazing fire. His feet were like bronze glowing in a furnace, and his voice was like the sound of rushing waters, and out of his mouth came a sharp double-edged sword. His face was like the sun shining in all its brilliance. Revelation 1:12-15

But the most amazing revelation, one that has been hidden for thousands of years, is that at the end of the 1,335 days – if we prepare now, during this time and age, for that great event, by purifying ourselves and putting on the white robes of the Children of Elahim – **we shall be like Him!** That is the blessing for you if you wait for and reach the end of the 1335 days.

From then on the world and its inhabitants will live and work in love, peace, joy, and hope. How could it be any other way, when millions of Sons of Elah walk the earth and petition their Father in Heaven on behalf of the People?

Epilogue

We examined many prophecies in this book; many you probably never read before. I encourage you go back and read again The Prophecy chapter starting on page 7. If you have read this far, you will see you now have more knowledge and understanding. Those few verses should now make more sense than when you first read them.

I awoke this morning at 4:30 and could not sleep. My head was filled with thoughts about this book and what it says. My mind also went back to the night of September 10, 2001. I read from Bloom's "The Lucifer Principle", the chapter "Are There Killer Cultures?" As I tried to go to sleep that night, I began to get restless, feeling that something ominous was about to happen. I tossed about until morning came when I felt like turning on the TV to see the news, but instead I couldn't. I *knew* that something happened. As I prepared for the day, my wife fixed breakfast and watched with disbelief as the planes slammed into the twin towers. I heard the sound of the news and knew that something was really wrong Just as I had feared: we were now at war.

Last night as I thought about these closing remarks I began to grasp, even more fully, the reality of what is in these pages. I saw that the Woman, the soon to be united Nation of Israel, has a deep and abiding relationship with her Husband, Eyahuwah. But she does know it. She has still continued her estrangement from His loving care.

I also saw how the People are the offspring of the relationship between Eyahuwah and the Woman. Only they do not know either their Father or their Mother. The People are off serving other gods – the gods of the nations that want to kill them.

Eyahuwah clothed the Woman with the sun and put the moon under her feet and placed the crown of 12 stars on her head, one star for each of her nations. These identified her with her Husband, and the People with their Father.

No other nation on earth has these Feasts and Holy Days on clean days as determined by the solar and Revealed Calendar given by their Father. But she chose to follow the nations round about her. She was not faithful. She became a prostitute and worse: *she* tried to *buy* favor from those with whom she slept. But these *lovers* only wanted to kill her and her offspring and to rob her of the great blessings she received from her ever-faithful Husband. So he divorced her and freed her from Him.

Eyahuwah turned to his Father the Lord of Spirits. Eyahuwah came in the flesh to die and pay the penalty his wife and her offspring had accrued. By death, He bought her and her offspring. He became a Son of Man descended from Judah and from King David. He died, was raised from the dead by His Father, and became a Son of God.

Now the offspring have a new Father in the Family of Elahim, Eyahushuah's Father, and a new Mother, His Mother, the Holy Spirit. The offspring can now become part of that Family, as Siblings to Eyahushuah (Eyahuwah). They can enter into Eternal Life now. And if they do, they can become like their Brother by being raised up from the dead. This "innumerable multitude" will appear in *new bodies* before their Father as Sons on the Feast of Firstfruits at the end of the 1,335 days according to the prophecy given to Daniel.

Imagine what kind of world it will be when millions of Sons of the Family of Elahim, bearing their Father's Name and power, walk the earth!

References

[Sept] The Septuagint with Apocrypha: Greek and English. Sir Lancelot C. L. Brenton, Grand Rapids, Michigan: Zondervan Publishing House, 1980.

Enoch, (The Ethiopic Apocalypse of). Translator, E. Isaac, Garden City, New York: Doubleday & Company, Inc., 1983.

Enoch, Book of: Together with a Reprint of the Greek Fragments, Ed. and translator, R. H. Charles. Kessinger Publishing, 1912.

[NAS] *New American Standard Bible, The Open Bible Edition*, The Lockman Foundation, La Habra, California. New York: Thomas Nelson, Publishers, 1978.

[NEB] Ed: Samuel Sandmel, *The New English Bible with the Apocrypha, Oxford Study Edition*, New York: Oxford University Press, 1976.

[NIV] *The Holy Bible, New International Version*, Grand Rapids, Michigan: Zondervan Bible Publishers, 1978.

[JSB] Ed: Adele Berlin and Marc Zvi Brettler. *The Jewish Study Bible*, Jewish Publication Society TANAKH Translation, New York: Oxford University Press, 2005.

The Catholic Encyclopedia Volume I, Copyright © 1907 by Robert Appleton Company, Online Edition Copyright © 2003 by K. Knight. http://www.newadvent.org/cathen/

The Upanishads, translated by Eknath Easwaran. Copyright © 1987 by the Blue Mountain Center of Meditation. Tomales, California: Nilgiri Press, 1996.

The Englishman's Hebrew and Chaldee Concordance of the Old Testament, Fifth Edition. London: Samuel Bagster and Sons, Limited.

The Englishman's Greek Concordance of the New Testament, Ninth Edition. London: Samuel Bagster and Sons, Limited.

Ed: James Donnegan, M. D. *A New Greek and English Lexicon ...*, First American, from the Second London Edition, Revised and enlarged by R. B. Patton. Boston: Hilliard, Gray & Co., 1840.

Ed: R. H. Charles, D.Litt., D.D. *The Apocrypha and Pseudepigrapha of the Old Testament in English, Volume II, Pseudepigrapha. Oxford: Oxford University Press, 1979.

The Holy Scriptures of the Old Testament, Hebrew and English, The British & Foreign Bible Society, 1997.

The Book of Jubilees, From the Ethiopic, A reprint from an edition published by E. J. Goodrich, Oberlin, Ohio, 1888. Thousand Oaks, California: Artisan Sales, 1980.

Metalogos, The Gospels of Thomas & Philip & Truth, Ecumenical Coptic Project, www.metalog.org, Athens, 2005.

The Complete Gospels, Annotated Scholars Version, Robert J. Miller, Ed., Sonoma, California: Polebridge Press, 1994.

Ed: James H. Charlesworth. The Old Testament Pseudepigrapha, Volume 1, Apocalyptic Literature and Testaments, Garden City, New York: Doubleday & Company, Inc., 1983.

Ed: James H. Charlesworth. The Old Testament Pseudepigrapha, Volume 2, Expansions of the "Old Testament" and Legends, Wisdom and Philosophical Literature, Prayers, Psalms, and Odes, Fragments of Lost Judeo-Hellenistic Works, Garden City, New York: Doubleday & Company, Inc., 1985.

Enoch, The Book of or 1 Enoch. Ed. and translator R. H. Charles. Oxford: Clarendon Press, 1912.

The Scriptures. Northriding, Republic of South Africa: Institute for Scripture Research, www.messianic.co.za, 2006.

Michael J. Behe, Darwins Black Box, The Biochemical Challenge to Evolution. New York: Touchstone, 1998.

Howard Bloom, The Lucifer Principle, A Scientific Expedition into the Forces of History. New York: Atlantic Monthly Press, 1995.

Yair Davidi, Ephraim, The Gentile Children of Israel, Revised Edition. Jerusalem, Israel: Russell-Davis Publishers, 2001.

Yair Davidiy, Joseph, The Israelite Destiny of America, 2nd Edition. Jerusalem, Israel: Russell-Davis Publishers, 2004

Paul Davies, The Mind of God, The Scientific Basis for a Rational World, New York: Simon and Schuster, 1992.

Bart D. Ehrman, Misquoting Jesus, The Story Behind Who Changed the Bible and Why, San Francisco, California: HarperSanFrancisco, 2005.

Bart D. Ehrman, Lost Scriptures, Books that Did Not Make It into the New Testament, New York: Oxford University Press, 2003.

Bart D. Ehrman, Lost Christianities: The Battles for Scripture and Faith We Never Knew,

New York: Oxford University Press, 2003.

Helen Ellerbe, *The Dark Side of Christian History*, San Rafael, California: Morningstar Books, 1995.

Everett Fox, *The Five Books of Moses*, The Schoken Bible, Volume 1, New York: Random House, 1997.

Graham Hancock. *Underworld, The Mysterious Origins of Civilization*, New York: Three Rivers Press, 2002.

Sam Harris. *The End of Faith; Religion, Terror, and the Future of Reason*, New York, New York: W. W. Norton & Company, Inc, 2004.

Jonathan Kirsch, *God Against the Gods, The History of the War Between Monotheism and Polytheism*, New York: Viking Compass, 2004.

James L. Kugel. *The Bible as it was*, Cambridge, Massachusetts, and London, England: The Belknap Press of Harvard University, 1997.

Paul LaViolette. *Earth Under Fire, Humanity's Survival of The Apocalypse*, Schenectady, New York: Starburst Publications, 1997.

Leonora Leet. *The Secret Doctrine of the Kabbalah, Recovering the Key to Hebraic Sacred Science*, Copyright © 1999 by Leonora Leet. Rochester, Vermont: Inner Traditions, 1999.

Garcia Martinez. *Qumran and Apocalyptic*, Leiden, The Netherlands: Brill, E. J., 1992.

Garcia Martinez. *The Dead Sea Scrolls Translated, The Qumran Texts in English*, Pubs: Leiden, Netherlands: E. J. Brill; Grand Rapids, Michigan: Wm. B. Eerdmans Publishing Company, 1996.

Emil Schürer. *A History of the Jewish People in the Time of Jesus*, New York, New York, Schocken Books, Inc., 1941.

Lee Strobel. *The Case for a Creator, A Journalist Investigates Scientific Evidence That Points Toward God*, Grand Rapids, Michigan: Zondervan, 2004.

Wikipedia contributors, "Medes," *Wikipedia, The Free Encyclopedia*, http://en.wikipedia.org/w/index.php?title=Medes&oldid=78316419 (accessed September 28, 2006).

Wikipedia contributors, "Persians," *Wikipedia, The Free Encyclopedia*, http://en.wikipedia.org/w/index.php?title=Persians&oldid=33930152 (accessed September 28, 2006).

Yagel Yadin. *Bar-Kokhba, The rediscovery of the legendary hero of the last Jewish Revolt against Imperial Rome*, Jerusalem, Israel: Steimatzky's Agency Ltd., 1978

BLOG: "Lift Up Your Voice!"

To keep up with the news and changes coming in our spiritual life, make it your habit to visit the Lift Up Your Voice! blog site at :

http://innertech.wordpress.com.

Each week new articles by Dr. Timothy Sakach, Ph. D. are published as a message to the world in this transitional time. There will come turmoil around the globe as the end of this age rapidly approaches its prophesied demise, while at the same time, the force of the coming new Age of Righteousness reaches deeply into the spiritual life of all people to prepare them for what will surely come.

COMMENTS FROM READERS OF THE BLOG:
On "Spiritual Discernment" ...
> *You're insights on this issue are so accurate that I don't even know how to comment. Thank you so much for posting this.*

On "ELAH, ELAHIM, EYAHUWAH: Restoring the Greatest Names" ...
> *I too am convinced (after studying countless related Scriptural passages) of the importance of the unfolding mystery shrouding the name of God; in fact, I believe it to be the key to the whole of Scripture .*

On the Jesus Tomb Controversy ...
> *If those bones belonged to Jesus, you are right; it would not mean that He didn't rise, but that he shed his body, like a "kernel" of wheat would in order to grow into a different body. Thanks for your interesting post.*

This blog is fast becoming one of the most powerful and sought after sources of spiritual information in the world. New articles and controversies stir up the mind and spirit to set people free from the shackles of religious tyranny and control.

One of our greatest tasks in life is know the truth and make it our own. But it is not easy to do. There is so much flack flying around that everyone gets hurt by it. Truth is tough. Nothing can hurt it. Even liars and deceivers cannot change the truth. But if we are not careful, they might change our minds and thoughts.

I must present you with the truth that was recorded long ago for our benefit. This is an awesome task. If what I tell you is wrong, then I will be held accountable for it, in the same way that the preachers of "damnation" will be. But if I tell you the truth, then I have done my job. Whether to believe it or not is your job. I cannot use trickery, or fancy stories, or scare tactics. Furthermore, I must provide you with references to what I received and used. Then you can check these things out for yourself.

Timothy Sakach, From "RESURRECTION: Part 2 - Make Ready for the Change."

www.ingramcontent.com/pod-product-compliance
Lightning Source LLC
Chambersburg PA
CBHW030141170426
43199CB00008B/154